Streams

IN THE

Desert

*Healing Letters for the
Wounded Heart*

Steve Porter

Deeper Life
PRESS

Dedicated to the many spiritual wounded warriors on the battlefield. It is not over; God is not finished with you. May His healing presence wrap around you and give you a fresh start.

**"The Lord is close to the brokenhearted;
he rescues those whose spirits are crushed."**

(Psalm 34:18)

With his heart still pounding

the son cautiously approached the Father with his face filled with shame

yet his Father was already running to meet him

They embraced

They wept

The son asked for work

but the father was not listening

He was dancing to another tune

Amazing Grace, how sweet the sound!

Acknowledgements

Special thanks to our editors and publishing team, Nancy Arant Smith, Matt Rowland, Ken Darrow, M.A. and Sarah Lewis.

Special thanks most of all to our Beloved Daddy God, who holds us so close in the palm of His hand.

TABLE OF CONTENTS

Introduction

[handwritten annotations: "As per Dang Addison Praise God! on 10/15/22 prophetic word for a Lord, drink of Living Water." "Ask the"]

Even good soldiers might take 'bullets' and collapse in defeat or disgrace. In the same way, millions of men and women in our world have been injured in spiritual warfare and are now lying wounded on the field. They are thirsty for a refreshing stream, to take a drink from the living water. God is raising up 'medics'—healers who are equipped with compassion and grace. Wounded warriors need grace-driven stretcher bearers, healers, and cheerleaders who believe in restoration and healing and are committed to helping them rise to fight again. It's our desire for this book to do just that!

The enemy who entraps the vulnerable can be overthrown, but we must also have a strategy to rescue those taken hostage or left wounded on the battlefield. God has a loving message of healing and restoration for His church: **"I will never give up on you, no matter how desperate your need. I am here for you, with a plan to raise you up."**

The creed of the Army Rangers is, "Never shall I fail my comrades ... I will never leave a fallen warrior to fall into the hands of the enemy." If only the army of Christian soldiers would care for their brothers and sisters in the same way.

1

The stark truth is that when one of us is wounded the whole body is wounded. When one is disabled, the others should be there to nurse him back to health. Just like the ranger motto, ours should read: "You go in together, you stick together, and you come out together. If you can't come out together, don't bother coming out." If believers would live by this motto, the world would be a different place entirely!

She could see no way out when she asked herself, **"How am I going to get through this? I can't see a glimmer of hope in any direction. In fact, I'm not sure I'll survive it at all."**

Does this sound familiar? Have you ever felt like it would take a miracle to untangle your mess? Most Christians are familiar with the promises of God to draw near to those in trouble. And yet they may sound trite and inadequate, like a pat answer instead of a comfort when the heat is on. You can't help but wonder, "How can God make anything good out of the mess I've made?"

Are you aware that if you combine oil with ashes and soak it in a salt brine solution, you'll end up with a type of scum that rises to the top? If you put the scum under pressure, it becomes a bar of soap. What appeared to be little more than waste is, in fact, a product with many great benefits.

In the same way, if you combine the ashes of your shattered life with the anointing oil of heaven, and mix it with the salt of bitter tears, it, too, will become something valuable. And our loving God is not only able but quite willing to work out the details of this miraculous equation, so that it becomes something beautiful in the end, if only you hold on to your dreams.

In this book you will find letters written by myself to minister to your personal needs. We recommend that you read all the letters slowly and prayerfully and carefully considering each one. It is our hope that in the process you will have an encounter with the Holy Spirit, our amazing Comforter. If you have untreated wounds, open your heart to our loving God as you think on these things, letting Him apply His healing ointment and sooth you with His love. He's waiting with open arms to welcome you home. May these letters be like a refreshing stream in that desert place.

Read on...

PLEASE GOD! ✓ 10/16/22

Rescue

me!

"You went out to rescue your chosen people, to save your anointed ones..." (Habakkuk 3:13)

Dear Precious One,

Have you ever been in need of rescue? Perhaps you made some really poor choices and now you are paying the piper for them. Stress has been mounting as the consequences have come home to roost in your life.

Are you weak and perhaps even lying wounded on the field of conflict, unable to fight 'the good fight of faith' another day?

Are you a fallen warrior, wounded from the result of the dreadful mistakes you've made?" I see your scars, and the heartache written on your face. Shame and guilt plague you like rude uninvited guests who refuse to leave.

Or perhaps you're lying curled in fetal position on the battlefield through no fault of your own, but you have fallen victim to the ravages of life situations. And while it's not your fault, you're still in need of rescue.

To both of you, the duped and the victim, my message is the same. The Lord is your strength and He will rescue you! Did He not leave the ninety-nine for the one who wandered? He has not abandoned you! He is coming even now with the power of His right hand!

Psalms 20:6 declares: "Now this I know: The LORD gives victory to his anointed. He answers him from his heavenly sanctuary with the victorious power of his right hand."

Exodus 15:2 also points out: "The LORD is my strength and my defense; he has become my salvation. He is my God, and I will praise him, my father's God, and I will exalt him."

He will rescue His anointed ones. If you repent and walk in humility before the Lord, He will not cast you aside. He will release you from the prison of your past! If you are a victim, He has not forgotten you or left you to suffer alone. You will not be left on a field of battle with no prospect of rescue.

Here He comes, Our Father, with eyes full of love and compassion. He approaches you, unafraid to gently bandage your wounds and to meet your need, to heal you wherever you hurt. He's not afraid to get dirty or risk associating with you when you're down and out. Our God will stand with you through your brokenness or in the awkward silence of the night season. He will love you with each and every step you make toward wholeness. He will silence your accusers while pouring into your wound the healing oil of the Holy Spirit so you can be made whole! In fact, God is waiting, inclining His ear to hear your prayer and to run to your rescue.

"God is our refuge and strength, an ever-present help in trouble. 2Therefore we will not fear, though the earth give way and the mountains fall into the heart of the sea, 3though its waters roar and foam and the mountains quake with their surging." (Psalms 46:1-3)

Dear God. RESCUE me! I am in need of your healing touch. I am amazed by You, Jesus! You are always that kind of faithful friend. You took stones away from the hands of the angry mob. You touched lepers and healed them. You threw homecoming parties for prodigals. You granted thieves paradise and you will RESCUE, RESTORE and REVIVE my soul. You are my REFUGE and my strength.

[Handwritten note: HalleluYah! 10/18/22 The Lord spoke to me this morning! He has officially rescued me — "It is over" 49 years of demonic attack and satanic takeover OVER]

Torn Nets and Broken Pottery

"But the pot he was shaping from the clay was marred in his hands; so the potter formed it into another pot, shaping it as seemed best to him."(Jeremiah 18:4)

Dear Precious One,

Perhaps your life has been shattered, damaged, or even destroyed. If that's the case I have inspiring news for you. Our God is a God of restoration. Let's look at the definition of the word **'restoration'.** One definition is 'to mend', as in the mending of a broken net or even adding new cords to strengthen it.

Commercial fishermen seldom throw away a damaged net; instead they mend it or add new cords to reinforce it. In much the same way, when a broken life needs 'mending' we must use the healing oil of the Holy Spirit and the Word of God to reach out with the unconditional love of God to restore, to mend and to heal the broken spirit.

It's like the broken pottery spoken of in Jeremiah.

The Lord does not throw away the marred clay. Instead He warms it and places it back on the wheel to be shaped and molded again. Genuine restoration assists in the mending of that which has been broken.

Another aspect of restoration alludes to the *resetting of bone* that has been broken or is *out of joint*. I know firsthand this is an exceptionally painful experience, but one that is required for healing to take place. God does not tell us we should take a dislocated member who has been hurt or bruised and amputate him, rather He encourages us to restore him, to put him back in place so that the body can function normally again. God's way has always been to remove the sin, not the sinner. We, as believers, must lovingly receive and restore those who return to God in humble repentance for their failures.

The prostitute is looking for a church that will open its doors with a message of rescue instead of an attitude of disgust; the pregnant teenager is looking for a church that will open its arms with compassion instead of humiliation; those whose lives are wrecked because of adultery are looking for a church that will open its heart with forgiveness and healing instead of disdain. The sanctuary must become a place where people can come as they are and be loved and restored. It must become a place where we can be real.

Wounded warriors everywhere are looking for a church that offers compassion, deliverance, and healing. Child of God, maybe you're in need of God's loving restoration. Maybe your life is 'broken' and needs to be 'mended' by the Holy Spirit. Because of His great love He desperately wants to strengthen you and 'reset' your life! Every place where your life has become 'out of joint'—out of sync with His Spirit—He is more than willing to bring healing and restoration, making all things brand new. It only requires that we come to the end of our own abilities and ask Him to take control. – *I am here now, I can do nothing*

10/18/22

Restoration includes forgiveness, compassion, protection, covering, correction, discipline and deliverance. All of these, my precious one, are available to you if you ask. Your net may need mending or you may be shattered like a broken pot, but God has *not* forgotten you! In fact, Scripture says you're *always* on His mind, and He anxiously waits for you to come to Him so He can put your life back together again. Once you run back to Him, the Master Potter molds you into a vessel of honor.

Trust Him to do what you can't, to give you a future and hope you've never dared to imagine, because He wants that for you, even more than you do. And once you let Him take control, I promise you'll never be the same again.

Let my life offer compassion, deliverance, and healing to those that are broken and in need of mending. You have not forgotten me and neither will I forget others that desperately need rescue, restoration, and revival. I also thank you that you will heal me every place that I hurt. You are the great - I AM.

Thank You God, for loving me!

Jesus Wept

"And [he] said, Where have ye laid him? They said unto him, Lord, come and see. Jesus wept. Then said the Jews, Behold how he loved him!" (John 11:34-36)

Dear Precious One,

Jesus had a very special bond with friends Mary, Martha, and Lazarus; they weren't just casual acquaintances. We can catch a glimpse of His nature by observing the way He became intimately involved in their lives. And nothing has changed. Jesus still has a yearning to be close to His people today. In fact, we see into the heart of Jesus through the two most powerful words in the entire Bible, found in John 11:35: **"Jesus wept."**

He was not weeping for Lazarus, but rather for Mary and Martha. He so loved them that He shed tears of empathy; His heart ached because of their deep sorrow. I genuinely believe that every tear you shed also runs down the cheek of Jesus! He weeps today as you're drowning in the depths of grief. He says, "Oh, how I love you! I want to hold you in my arms and whisper that it will be okay." Can you feel the heartbeat of God for you? He loves you that much! You are that special to Him. Even the hairs on your head are numbered. You are that precious! I love my children more than life itself, but I can't tell you how many hairs are on their heads. Jesus can!

Not only does He love us as much as I love my children, but He loves us more than any earthly father ever could, because He doesn't just show love, He is love. Everything that love is, God is. When He looks at His children, He looks with a heart filled with love and tender compassion; He weeps over the things that so deeply affect His children.

Dear friend, if you're in pain right now, the most powerful medicine for you is the knowledge that Jesus cares for you in your struggle and that He weeps with you! He loves you. You have a purpose and a destiny, and you can be encouraged knowing He has not forgotten you.

Grab hold of the following Scriptures and meditate on them, allowing them to minister to your pain:

"The Lord *is* nigh unto them that are of a broken heart; and saveth such as be of a contrite spirit." (Psalm 34:18)

"He healeth the broken in heart, and bindeth up their wounds." (Psalm 147:3)

There is no wound so great that He cannot heal it; He will put the broken pieces of your life back together again, and make you a vessel of honor, better than before. I once heard someone say, "I'm a mess, Lord, but I'm your mess!" He will always show Himself incredibly faithful, but because He actually draws near to the brokenhearted, He is actually the closest when tragedy strikes. So run into His loving embrace and let His comfort meet your needs. He's waiting...

Lord, you care for me in my struggle and you weep when I weep! Thank you for your divine love. I have a purpose and a destiny, and you have not forgotten me.

Helpless

"Who is this coming up from the wilderness leaning on her beloved?" (Song of Solomon 8:5a)

Dear Precious One,

Do you ever feel helpless when battles overwhelm you—almost like you're floating in midair, with the ground far beneath your feet? Perhaps that's the way God likes things ... because when we feel helpless we must totally rely on Him. Like a child depending on its parents to supply, we lean on Him to provide the things we think we need.

At times we feel as if we're wrestling with a giant far beyond our ability to cope and we're desperate for God and His wisdom. So let me encourage you not to jump off the ship of expectation, simply because you're feeling insecure and weak.

Perhaps you feel as if you're kicking in midair with no sure footing, nothing but the cool breeze blowing against you. Remember you are His little child looking to your heavenly Daddy to tell you what to do. You cry out, "I'm your little child! Jesus, I need your wise words. Make a way for me!"

Just when we feel that we have our feet planted on solid ground, life challenges can lift us far above our own abilities and false confidence. In midair our feet search for solid ground and our arms flail, helpless to save ourselves.

In answer to our cries, we suddenly see with perfect vision, and know we are upheld by His arms, and He will not let go of us. When we thought we were all alone, defenseless, and circumstances were running us around in circles, our precious Savior held us close to His breast, calming all our fears, and assuring us of a blessed future.

This stunning revelation can lead us to a place of divine peace, knowing God has everything under control. This is the place where faith is born.

The Bible says, "**to be content in all things.**" (Phil. 4:11) Why is this so hard? Today many people allow anxiety to rule their hearts and lives, consumed by worry and "what if's. They get so caught up in tomorrow that they cannot enjoy today.

Many times we have unrealistic expectations, feeling as if we should always be on the mountain top, surrounded by gentle streams and lush, green grass. But the reality is that seasons come and go, and if we live long enough we'll face situations that are completely out of our control. At such times we will know we're out of our league and totally helpless.

Ask yourself these questions: What if it doesn't get better right away? Will I be as Paul and be content in all things? Consider this: though it was the last thing Jesus wanted to do, He chose to bear the cross and suffer a terrible, humiliating death for our benefit. He didn't feel like doing God's will any more than we do at times. But just like Jesus, we simply can't go by our feelings or we will be ruled and defeated by the flesh, failing to live out our destiny.

We should want our flesh to die in order to be filled and ruled by the Spirit and His leadership, in order to glorify God. And if we can believe there is some higher purpose in the trials we face, we can be thankful and have peace of mind, knowing that all is well with our souls and that God is still on the throne, pleased with us. What more could a child of God want!?

I cry out with all my heart "I'm your little child! Jesus, I need your wise words. Make a way for me!" My precious Savior, hold me close to your breast, calming all my fears, and assuring me of a blessed future. I place my trust in you!

Healing Presence

"In your presence is fullness of joy..."
(Psalms 16:11b)

Dear Precious One,

I want to tell you a secret you may never have heard before. There's a special place you can go that's so sweet and more real than mere words could ever express—a place that will cause you to raise your hands and fall to your knees, where you can't help but weep with great joy. In this special place you can bask in God's love and lie before His feet for hours on end. It's here where He draws near to you and imparts spirit and life into the dark, empty places inside you. It's a rare place where the very fire of heaven is released to work deep in the recesses of your soul.

In His presence you behold Him in His beauty. His face shines upon you and you see Him as He really is, a Father so in love with His precious child that He desires to do a miraculous healing work inside you.

"And the Lord came, and stood, and called as at other times, Samuel, Samuel. Then Samuel answered, Speak; for thy servant heareth."

(1 Samuel 3:10)

Did you get that? ***And the Lord came, and stood!*** Think about it! The Lord ***came*** and ***stood*** near Samuel and called him by name! Did you know, dear friend, that the Lord wants to come and ***stand*** beside you? He wants to reveal himself to you in a profound way through the presence of the Holy Spirit. I wish I could communicate with words what I am feeling as I write this... ***To think that the LORD HIMSELF would come and stand right beside me and call my name!*** That stunning revelation truly melts my heart!

"What is man, that thou art mindful of him? and the son of man, that thou visitest him?" *(Psalms 8:4)*

You are always on His mind. In fact, He wants nothing more than to come and visit you heart to heart in the person of His gentle Holy Spirit—in that place where time means nothing and nothing else matters. In that special place healing water flows and deep wounds are healed.

Perhaps you're carrying deep wounds, so deep no person could ever heal them, or maybe you're desperate for deliverance. You need bondages to break and chains to be shattered by the power of the Spirit. Or perhaps you have soul ties that only God can break once and for all. His healing presence is the place of release and freedom, where you fall at His feet and He comes to stand beside you.

I recall a season in my life where I sought the Lord, with nothing but the broken pieces of my damaged heart. It was there that I shared the depths of my brokenness and admitted my life was a mess, and that no one but Him could restore me. Man couldn't deliver me or heal my ugly scars. I was in a place of desperation when I stretched out on the basement floor and wept for hours that night, pleading with Him to come and touch my wounded soul. And He came, filling the room with His healing presence and gently laying His hand on me, healing every broken place, and making things brand new.

There in that secret place God's heart is overflowing with compassion for His weary, broken ones, eager to heal shattered lives and restore the things we lost when Adam sinned. All He asks is that we come and ask. He never says no, for His greatest desire is to reach out and touch those broken places. In His healing presence we discover the fullness of joy, and are made whole, with brand new hope and a future we can't even imagine. Embrace the secret place, dear friend, and be made whole!

LORD, come and stand right beside me and call my name. I give you my ears that I may listen to what is in your heart. I thank you for the secret place that is overflowing with compassion for me. I thank you that the weary and broken ones can find healing through your manifest presence. You are eager to heal shattered lives and restore all.

Never Too Late For a Resurrection

"Then he asked me, "Son of man, can these bones become living people again?" "O Sovereign Lord," I replied, "you alone know the answer to that."
(Ezekiel 37:3, NLT)

Dear Precious One,

Did you know that God is in every area of creation, even in those things that appear lifeless and dead? Just as a physician uses CPR (cardiopulmonary resuscitation) to breathe new life into patients in cardiac arrest, God is always standing by, ready to breathe new life into anything lifeless when we ask. He is there in our spiritual springtime and in the cold, winter months. And He is even closer, hovering nearby in our darkest hours, according to Psalm 34:18 where it says: **"The Lord is near to the brokenhearted and saves the crushed in spirit."**

The Ezekiel passage above asks the question, **"...can these bones become living people again?"** The word

19

'living' does not only mean to come back to life after being physically dead, it also applies to brokenness, a dying dream, a losing struggle, and times of hopelessness and despair in any area of our lives. 'To live' means to be refreshed, rejuvenated, revived, or to be given the promise of life. It also means to be restored or renewed—or simply to be made whole again.

Just as the wind breathed new life into the dry bones from the Ezekiel passage, God wants to resurrect our spirits as well. He wants to welcome us into His living presence and impart that same resurrection life to us, breathing new life into the dead places in our lives. And while some may come along and say God can't use us, God is saying otherwise, and His is the last word on the subject!

"Therefore prophesy and say unto them, Thus saith the Lord GOD; Behold, O my people, I will open your graves, and cause you to come up out of your graves, and bring you into the land of Israel." (Ezek. 37:12, NKJV)

Here God makes us a promise that He will bring us out of the darkness, opening our graves and allowing us to live again! We just have to listen and obey God's Word.

Are there areas of your life that need a touch of heaven? Ezekiel promises us that God is always watching, always ready to breathe new life into these dead and lifeless areas of our lives. When we face obstacles, we must realize that delays are only temporary. In fact, we must keep in mind that God is in charge, and He may be slowing things down a bit, in order for us to heal before breathing new life into our personal struggles so that we will truly fully receive the power and love of God.

To be 'resurrected' means far more than just bringing someone back to life. To be resurrected by the power of God makes us stronger, more mature and more powerful than we were before! **Did you hear that, Child of God?** *Stronger, more mature, and more powerful* **than ever before!**

And God always makes good on His promise of resurrection to anyone who belongs to Him. He alone can inject new life into dead places. All we have to do is ask, obey, wait, and receive.

Perhaps it will encourage you to understand the massive power of the resurrection. The term 'resurrection' means 'to stand up again'. This can be taken literally, to mean reviving an individual to a living state of consciousness, or it can be taken figuratively, as in reviving profound spiritual truths so we can experience God's tangible peace, joy, and love. And this can be applied to any area. There is no situation too hard for God to overcome—not physical death, not spiritual death, not emotional death. This same gift of the resurrection already resides in each and every one of us, as God's children, when His Spirit lives inside us.

"But if the Spirit of Him who raised Jesus from the dead dwells in you, He who raised Christ from the dead will also give life to your mortal bodies through His Spirit who dwells in you." (Romans 8:11, NKJV)

21

If God the Father was able to breathe new life into the lifeless body of His Son, then you and I are also beneficiaries of this great gift, given to us when Jesus died and was raised from the dead. But it's up to us to grab hold of this gift in faith, and believe it, as if it were so, because it only comes alive for us as we apply it and say, "It's mine, and I'm not taking no for an answer!" Once we do that we are supernaturally empowered and energized by the mighty power of God—unstoppable!

Psalm 84:11 says, **"No good thing does He withhold from those who walk uprightly."** That means that He will never refuse to restore to those who ask for help. No one is too far gone if they're still alive and breathing air. In fact, Psalm 116:2 (LB) puts it this way: **"Because He *bends down to listen*, I will pray as long as I have breath!"**

Jesus was raised from the dead by the power of God the Father, and that very same power already resides in us because His Holy Spirit lives inside us. With this inborn power, God can resurrect our dreams, our godly ambitions, and our passions. Every good thing that's been lost can be restored to even greater heights through the miraculous power of God.

Our dreams are like planted seeds. In order to sprout, they must first fall lifeless from the tree, be planted in the ground, and wait for springtime to arrive when they will begin to bloom and grow. And just as the sun rises every morning, we can depend on God's love to shine down to bring life to our dreams. Just as the sunshine impacts all living things, God promises us an abundant and fruitful life as we respond to His call to live again.

Have your dreams died? Perhaps you're holding them too tightly for God to do anything. We need to learn how to hold our dreams loosely, opening our hands and giving them to Him, understanding that sometimes dreams must die lest they consume us or become like idols—the driving force of our lives. In order for those dead dreams to actually live again, we must allow Him to make something from nothing.

According to Isaiah 61:1-3 —God is more than able to make beauty from ashes. But what if we ourselves lit the match that burned them to the ground? Will God still help us? Will He resurrect our dreams if we are the ones who caused them to die?

Absolutely! Because God is a God of the second chance. He takes joy and great delight in making all things new to bless us!

Do you have areas in your life where you feel dead inside? Are you struggling through personal issues, financial struggles, family problems, or a lack of passion for your career? Do you feel as if God has lost your address, forgotten about you, or is simply too busy to care?

Release the tight grip and open your hand, giving Him your worries, burdens, and dead or dying dreams. Let Him breathe new life into them for you.

Perhaps you feel unworthy of God's resurrection power

because of something you've done. Well, take heart, because if you humble yourself and repent, He will give beauty for ashes. Answer this question: Do you reject your precious children when they make mistakes? Of course not, and neither does God! He will lovingly correct you and then restore you back to health, making all things new!

The first step is to embrace the power of God, believing He will restore you. Ask Him to breathe new life into the dark and lifeless areas of your life. Be patient and wait in faith. Don't quit before the miracle happens! Hold on to the promise as if your life depended on it, because it does. And never take no for an answer!

God, you are more than able to make beauty from the ashes of my life. You are a God of the second chance. You take joy and great delight in making all things new! It is never too late for a resurrection in my life! Bring it on!

Wash Me in Your Presence

"Purify me from my sins, and I will be clean; wash me, and I will be whiter than snow." (Psalms. 51:7)

Dear Precious One,

Isn't it time you allowed the Lord to wash you clean? Your first love has been reduced to mere embers that need the Holy Spirit to once again blow them into a raging fire of holiness and passion. His presence cannot flourish in an atmosphere of carnality. You can't live with one foot in heaven and the other in hell. Let go and repent of every evil attitude, word and deed, in the name of Jesus.

Dear Friend, be that person of war against your fleshly appetites. A day of reckoning will soon come without warning when you will give an account, so give God permission to clean house in your heart. Open the locked doors to the dark corners and let Him shine light into every one! Perhaps you've struggled for years to break free from sin, but today is a new day! Ask the Spirit of God to burn out every stronghold of sin that remains. He will! In His presence we are purified! Rest in His holy presence and let Him transform you so that you may recover all.

My prayer is that you will begin to sense the Holy Spirit washing you right now—making you clean, renewing your mind, and making all things new. You can walk in freedom and boldly approach the throne through the shed blood of Christ. You are made righteous and clean by His work on the cross. Let go of the sin you've held so tightly, and once more embrace holiness.

Pray this prayer with me right now.

Wash me that I may be clean. *"Oh wretched man that I am."* (Romans *7:24*) *"My heart is deceitfully wicked above all things."* (Jeremiah 17:9) Only You, God, know how true this statement is. Search out and destroy anything in me that breaks your heart. Take it away, because it makes me sick, too!

Why do I repeatedly wound You with my sin? How can I not see the pain I cause you? *"Create in me a clean heart."* (Psalms 51:10) Take not your manifest presence from me. Life is not worth living apart from your presence. Forgive and change me. Restore me to that place of innocence before You.

It's true that once I repent you don't hold my offenses against me, but You hate the separation—the wall that sin builds between us to keep us apart. You desire to forgive, restoring the fellowship between us, and you keep *"no record of my wrongs."* (1 Corinthians 13:4) *"Your mercy is new every single morning,"* (Lamentations 3:22-23) and You offer grace even when I don't understand how. Let my transgression grieve me as deeply as it grieves You. Give me a holy hatred for my sin, and let my heart be yours alone.

Teach me your ways and help me obey You with all my heart. Direct my steps and tell me what to do; only then will I find great joy and endless delight. Turn my heart toward your statutes and away from selfish gain and self-love. Help me hate and turn away from worthless things, and preserve me according to your holy Word. Release into me a consuming desire for only You; purify me, and restore me.

In Jesus' name, Amen

May your unfailing love be mine always; I put my hope in you alone. I will walk in freedom, for You are my deliverer. I delight in your commands and love every one of them. Give me a heart that is willing, that I may always cling tightly to You, and hate foolish and evil things. May I turn my heart toward You today and forever, that I may know You intimately, and worship You unhindered.

Spiritual Lepers

"A man with leprosy came and knelt in front of Jesus, begging to be healed. "If you are willing, you can heal me and make me clean," he said.

41 Moved with compassion, Jesus reached out and touched him. "I am willing," he said. "Be healed!" 42 Instantly the leprosy disappeared, and the man was healed." (Mark 1:40-42)

Dear Precious One,

During Jesus' lifetime the most disfiguring and ghastly disease of its time was leprosy—a foul, highly-contagious, and usually fatal condition that was looked upon with terrible dread and repulsion. If anyone dared to touch a leper, he was almost sure to catch that hideous disease. Leprosy was caused by unclean habits.

The Book of Leviticus explains how they treated this disease. When someone thought they might have it they immediately went to a priest. According to Jewish law, leprosy had to be healed by God via a priest, rather than by a physician.

Unfortunately the only way to stop the spread of this disease was to isolate its victims. Leviticus 13:46 commands, **"All the days wherein the plague shall be in him he shall be** defiled; **he is unclean: he shall dwell alone; without the camp shall his habitation be."** The leper could no longer associate with the pure; he was cast into permanent exile, apart from the rest of his family and community.

He lived as an outcast, disfigured by a disease running rampant through his body. He ripped his clothes to express his extreme agony and anguish. He cried out for the mercy of God while his head was bare to express intense humiliation. He covered his upper lip and cried aloud, **"Unclean! Unclean!"** so that the undefiled would stay away and not risk contamination.

I can imagine how these lepers must have felt. They were looked upon with horror, torn away from those they loved, suddenly cast out of the camp never to return. People fled when they heard them coming, shouting, **"Unclean! Unclean!"** Can you imagine the desperate state of hopelessness that consumed a newly-diagnosed leper, knowing he had no future other than more torment, further disfigurement and certain death?

In Scripture, leprosy symbolizes sin, which infects the human spirit and spreads through our souls to defile the very fiber of our lives. Even today we have many spiritual lepers who have isolated themselves from the church because they are unclean. They are defiled by sin yet they feel abandoned and forsaken, with no one but themselves to blame. They want to be healed, and they are ready to repent. But the question they're asking is this: is there a cure?

We do not have to look any further than the life of Jesus for the answer. As the man with leprosy fell at the beautiful feet of our precious Master, and begged for mercy and healing, his face was probably severely disfigured and frightening, while the smell of rotting flesh filled the air and repulsed those nearby. Yet, Jesus' gentle face shined with compassion and empathy, when He reached out and touched him—an unthinkable act! Why risk associating with this unclean man, let alone touching his extremely contagious skin? Yet *He did!* Moved with deep compassion, Jesus reached out and touched him, and he was instantly made whole, ready to be restored to those he so desperately loved and missed!

Perhaps you feel much like that unclean leper. Because of disobedience you have become a spiritual leper and others are repulsed by the smell of your carnal flesh. You feel ugly inside, and are sick at heart that you no longer have a niche in the family of God. You are an outcast and live outside the camp. You are a defeated warrior lying curled up and overwhelmed on the battlefield.

If that describes you, I'm calling you out of your isolation; you're not to dwell alone another day! I see your pain and how your soul has become vexed because of the poor choices you've made. You contaminated your soul with the filth of this world and now you feel you can never be accepted again. And though you've asked God to forgive you, you believe you are too far gone to ever be forgiven, too lost to be found, and so you cry out "Unclean! Unclean!" You expect others to run away in disgust, because you're a spiritual leper.

But wait... I can see the scarred hand of our Precious Lord tenderly reaching out to you. I see the tears of compassion as He weeps for you. His teardrops fall gently upon your head as you lower your eyes in shame, afraid to even meet His gaze. The foul smell of your past still lingers upon you when He lifts your chin, and with eyes full of love He looks deep into your soul and says these amazing words... "Because you have repented and come back to Me, I have made you clean! I have made all things new. You are no longer a leper or an outcast ... instead you are my ***child***!"

When you, my Bridegroom, comes I will wear a white robe washed in the blood of the perfect Lamb. Thank you that your presence makes me bright. I Lay aside the garments that are stained with sin and shame and put on a new garment that is spotless and white. Lord, I thank you that I am called your child!

Restore

"I restore the crushed spirit of the humble and revive the courage of those with repentant hearts."
(Isaiah 57:15)

Dear Precious One,

Rise up, Child of God! Rise Up! Shake off that slumbering spirit—there is a mighty warrior within you that needs to awakenSubmit to God; make the choice today to become that Child of God, to honor God, and pursue virtue, purity, and holiness.

You say you've blown it big time and you're drowning in the mire of your poor choices? *Is it too late? Can God restore my heart? Can I once again walk in purity and holiness before the Lord?* YES, you can! YES, you will! YES, He is able! He is the God of the second chance! We all desperately need this revelation, so grab hold of it with all that's in you.

Begin today by letting go of your obsession with the past, where captives stay bound in the prison of their own making. Stop looking back with regret, and instead press on! Yes, PRESS ON! Press forward past the blunders of the past, press on through the guilt and the shame, and press on through the confusion and doubt. He is already standing there bidding you come to the secret place; He is ready to blot out your sins with His holy blood. He is ready to make all things new in your life. He is ready to restore your honor and give you a fresh, new start.

Your past may cause you to feel "crushed and overwhelmed" beyond your ability to endure, thinking you'll never get past it, yet humble yourself before your God! Stretch out on the floor, desperate before Him, and share your deepest desire for Him alone. Unload your heartache and brokenness at the foot of His cross and leave it there so He can raise you up brand new.

The Lord responds to a broken, humble heart, to a soul that knows how to repent and admit where it missed the mark. As we rid ourselves of layers of self-love, control and pride, we are clothed anew with the beauty of the Lord.

Child of God, He desires to restore you and revive your spirit. He desires for you to begin again. Let me say it once more: only humble yourself before the mighty hand of God and:

"...then the Lord your God will restore your fortunes. He will have mercy on you and gather you back from all the nations where he has scattered you." (Deuteronomy 30:3)

I say again, you no longer need to hang your head with guilt and shame; once you have confessed and forsaken your sin, **you are a brand new creation in Christ Jesus**, and through His shed blood He has made you righteous. And when the devil comes to accuse you of things you've done in the past, use your authority to tell him he's talking to the wrong person, because you are a blood-washed child of God. When you stand up to him and testify to what Jesus did, Satan will have to flee, because the only power he has against you is when he can convince you his lies are true. Refuse to believe a negative word, because Jesus took *everything* to the cross, and wants to restore to us everything that was lost when Adam sinned. Live as if it is so, because it is!

Because of your longing and love for Him, you will walk in the Spirit again as you pursue faithfulness to Him alone, giving Him first place in your life. Picture this: He gently calls your name, and you approach the Lord. Rays of splendor pour from his hands and heart, and His face shines with a love so pure it drives you to tears; His voice is like the sound of many waters running through your soul when He sings a song of rejoicing over the very day you were born, and His presence captivates you with incredible joy and peace.

He says over you even now:

"I am your Father... You are my child... I have never stopped loving you, even while you were turned away. Because you have humbled yourself and repented I will restore all that locusts have eaten, and through my blood you are made whole!"

Even so, Lord, let it be... I press forward past the blunders of the past; I press on through the guilt and the shame, and press on through the confusion and doubt. I thank you that you are already standing there bidding me to come to our secret place.

Restore me

Sons of Mercy

"Where is another God like you, who pardons the sins of the survivors among his people? You cannot stay angry with your people forever, because you delight in showing mercy."
(Micah 7:18)

Dear Precious One,

The people of Israel were oftentimes wayward, regularly wandering off track and missing the mark by a country mile. In fact, the first time Moses came down from the mountain the people were worshiping a golden calf while the Lord stood by, a deserted lover. And while He could've reacted in fury and destroyed them all with a word, that didn't happen. Rather, He once again met Moses on the mountain in order to restore the covenant with those He loved. The sheer fact that Exodus 34 was written is evidence that He is a God of mercy and grace rather than a God who rushes to judgment.

The first covenant God made on the mountain went like this: **"If you will obey my voice and keep my covenant,** you shall be my own possession among all peoples; for all the earth is mine, and you shall be to me a kingdom of priests and a holy nation." (Ex. 19:5-6). What an incredible promise! But instead of remaining loyal and worshiping the one true God, they abandoned a relationship with Him to worship a golden cow made with their own wayward hands. They had deserted the God of all mercy.

These people had a long track record of sin and disobedience that included their lack of faith at the Red Sea, bitter complaints against God in the wilderness, and finally worshiping a golden calf!

What is most revealing in this story is not the fact that God is willing to meet with Moses again and renew their promises to one another, but that Exodus 34:5 says: **"The Lord descended in the cloud and stood with Moses there, and proclaimed the name of the Lord."**

God declares in verse 6: **"Yahweh! Yahweh!"** and then explains the meaning of His name, in words so descriptive that even New Testament descriptions can't compare. **"A God merciful and gracious, slow to anger, and abounding in steadfast love and faithfulness, keeping steadfast love for thousands, forgiving iniquity and transgression and sin."**

I am convinced that the Lord has more patience with us than we can ever imagine—certainly far more than we have with each other. We often have a zero-patience policy with others and are quick to execute them with our tongues and regard them as worthless. We are, however, extremely long-suffering with our own flaws, faults and shortcomings, excusing ourselves with: "God knows my heart... I didn't mean it that way... He loves me just the way I am..." or, "I am a work in progress."

Luke Chapter 9 tells us that Jesus was headed toward Jerusalem, where he didn't take the most direct route, but instead went through Samaria. He sent several friends ahead to arrange for overnight accommodations, but the people who lived there refused to welcome Jesus. James and John were infuriated when they heard the news and bellowed, **"Lord, do you want us to call fire down from heaven and destroy them [even as Elijah did]?"** (Luke 9:54) I believe that verbal explosion is what earned James and John the nickname 'Sons of thunder'. These guys essentially asked permission to nuke that little Samaritan village! As we read on Jesus gently rebukes them, explaining that His mission is to heal and transform rather than to assault or annihilate.

It's intriguing to read this incident as recorded in Luke 9 and then move on to Acts Chapter 8, where it says that after Jesus' ascension Christianity began to multiply like wildfire through the villages of Samaria. When that happened, the church in Jerusalem sent Peter and John to minister to the new believers there. Well, can you envision how John reacted ... now that he was far more mature in his walk with Christ? You have to wonder how he responded upon arriving in that village full of new believers, in a place where, years earlier, his anger had made him want to wipe them out!

I believe that, oftentimes, we as Christians become sons of thunder, quick to judge others, strict and rigidly critical, while we judge ourselves by our good intentions. We refuse to cut others any slack and want God to deal quickly and harshly with those we perceive as evil or hopeless.

I am discovering that God is far more merciful than I. I pray that I too will learn to show mercy and compassion, because God has given those things to me, undeserving as I am. Now that doesn't mean we are to wink and excuse sin or that we compromise in any way, but rather that we remain steadfast, hoping for the best and praying that God's love will transform even the hardest of hearts. We hope for a fallen wounded warrior's total restoration and recovery. If we are overflowing with the love of God we will never give up on others, but will know that nothing, absolutely nothing is impossible with God.

Scripture tells us that the God of Israel is the same **"yesterday, today and forever."** (Hebrews 13:8) He never misrepresented His nature, even to accommodate human beings. He is exactly who He always was, a just, fair and merciful God and Father to His beloved. His patience and tender mercies are evident throughout the Old Testament, just as His love and judgment are also apparent in the New.

The God of both mercy and judgment awaits each of us at the end of our journey. He always extends His hand in restoration to those who will repent and humble their hearts. Scripture tells us that there is a remnant of believers on Earth who possess the same tender mercy toward others, who are quick to love and forgive, ready to believe God's best and to mourn when judgment falls on the wicked. And lest we forget, if it weren't for His unmerited grace and forgiveness, we too would be condemned. Because we will all stand before God and give an account of how we behaved in the flesh, we must bask in the manifest love of Christ, letting Him transform us, so that we are full to running over with the fruit of the spirit, quick to sow mercy so that we may also reap mercy on judgment day.

Dear Lord, help us to be sons of mercy rather than sons of thunder! I pray for my fellow warriors who have fallen in the field. Restore them! Heal them! Deliver them! "Where is another God like you, who pardons the sins of the survivors among his people? You cannot stay angry with your people forever, because you delight in showing mercy."

I WANT MORE

"Choosing rather to suffer affliction with the people of God, than to enjoy the pleasures of sin for a season." (Hebrews 11:25)

Dear Precious One,

Let this prayer saturate your soul and each word come forth with power and presence, for God will draw near to you as you pursue Him. I would encourage you to pray this prayer several times a week. And as you do, may you receive a greater desire for more of God.

"Father God, I want more than the passing pleasures of this life! Your servant Moses refused to be called a son of Pharaoh and chose rather to endure the pain of suffering. He embraced the affliction of his flesh and valued heavenly treasure rather than enjoy the fleeting pleasures of sin for a season.

"Whatever rested in the heart of Moses place that in me even now! I want more than the temporary, fleeting desires of sin and the flesh. I refuse to be called a child of this world; rather I am a child of the living God, bought with a holy price, set apart for Your purposes. I am Your warrior.

"My heart is deceitful and wicked, more than capable of entertaining the pleasures of sin, but I want more! More than what I have right now, more than this world could ever offer me. I want You. Your eyes that blaze with holy fire; Your face that shines brighter than a noon day sun; the beauty of Your splendor that surrounds me even now. Give me more, Lord. I want more.

"Grant me the grace to overcome the hidden traps and deceitful illusions of the enemy. For his illusions are full of deception, wrapped in false promises for fulfillment, but leaving his prey shattered and alone. I want more.

"I thank You that, even when I stray, You never abandon me. You stand there patiently, quietly anticipating my return to Your arms. You are not a God who can forsake His child, for You are good. I will taste and see the goodness of my God every day of my life.

"You are washing my mind, purging my soul, and purifying my innermost being. Do Your deep work within my heart even as I lay at Your feet. I surrender the passing pleasures of this life. I surrender, because I love You more. More than life itself, more than the air I breathe—more than anything.

"This affliction of the flesh—let me embrace it as a love gift to you. Let me lay it all down with sweet surrender. Did you not willingly and lovingly lay it all down for me?

Did you not endure the cross that I may have You? You suffered the shame and vulnerability of the whip and the crown. You stood there alone ... deserted by those closest to You.

"Even now, I choose to suffer affliction with the people of God, rather than enjoy the pleasures of sin for a season! For I do not stand alone; You stand with me through it all. Your grace and Your love are forever mine."

Whatever rested in the heart of Moses place that in me even now! I want more than the temporary, fleeting desires of sin and the flesh. I refuse to be called a child of this world; rather I am a child of the living God, bought with a holy price, set apart for Your divine purposes.

Attitude

"Let this mind (attitude) be in you, which was also in Christ Jesus." (Philippians 2:5)

Dear Precious One,

This word 'mind' is literally translated as 'attitude'. When we're going through hard times and facing struggles the first thing we tend to do is adopt a negative attitude. Some people boldly wear T-shirts that say, "I love my attitude problem" or put a bumper sticker on their car that says, "Attitude". Sometimes attitude is written all over them, and you can see it in their body language. The problem with a bad attitude is that it can be contagious. If we don't keep our focus on God, we can often catch a bad attitude from someone else.

When your attitude is negative and filled with doubt the whole world stinks; it doesn't matter how beautiful the flowers are. A hardened attitude is like a dreadful disease. It causes us to close our minds and throw away our faith, and that leads to a dark future—a self-fulfilling prophecy that can only cycle downward.

When we face hard times we often become angry, and if we can't physically hit someone, we lash out at the first target that presents itself. Nine out of ten people who fail do so because of their attitudes and not their lack of abilities. We need to remember that God chooses us based on how teachable we are. The reality is that we dare not trust those with bad attitudes because we never know how they will react. The Lord can't trust someone who is not a vessel of honor, teachable and obedient. If you want to alter your life, you must change your attitude. If you're sick of the way things are going, you have to change the way you deal with things on the inside first. Only you can master your moods; only you can tame your temper, and that can only be when we yield to the power of the Holy Spirit.

Some people excuse their behavior during times of stress by saying, "Oh, I have an Irish temper and I can't help myself." But the problem is that, if they don't change, it can affect their entire future, because their attitudes precede them wherever they go and can actually predict where they'll end up. Our lives are 10% what happens to us and 90% how we react to those events. How do you react when you face difficult struggles?

Your attitude will affect your circumstances and cause you to either soar, or to crash. Your attitude actually goes much further than mere facts. Some people excuse their behaviors with, "Well, the fact is blah-blah-blah, and that's why I have such a bad attitude." But your attitude will actually dictate the outcome if you choose to walk in faith rather than acting out of your negative emotions. Do you want to move that mountain? Then you must do what pleases God and choose to give your anger to Him and adopt a good attitude—faith.

Are you aware that your attitude is far more important than your past? Many people use the following excuse, "Well, I have a bad attitude because of the things I've been through. It's a normal reaction to stress." But the attitudes you choose will make or break your situation. And whether it feels like it or not, *it's your choice* whether to become bitter or better. It's your choice whether to stand in faith or fall into doubt. However, I want to remind you of something very important: If you choose doubt and bitterness, you open the door to the enemy to wreak havoc in every part of your life. But when you stand in faith, you release God and His angels to work on your behalf—to do things you can't even dream of!

Father, change my attitude and give me the mind of Christ. Help me to master my moods and tame my temper, as I yield to the power of the Holy Spirit.

Closer

"Then all his disciples deserted him and ran away."
(Mark 14:50)

Dear Precious One,

Even as a perfect and sinless man Jesus was abandoned by those He loved best. The ones into whom He poured Himself most were the first to run away when things got tough. He prayed alone in the garden, facing His darkest hour without help or support from his closest friends.

If Jesus, the perfect Son of God, was able to face His darkest hour alone, is there a way for you to stand strong though alone, when your world comes crashing down? Those around you may not be spiritually mature enough to offer support in your time of need, so they abandon you. Others may be so overwhelmed with their own issues that they, too, tend to disappear when you need them most.

When our situations are no longer appealing, and we have nothing left to give, who will be left to stand with us?

We will never know who our true friends are until we

experience failure and loss. A humiliating blow will separate your true friends from mere followers.

Followers will follow you when you're winning and there's something to be gained from the relationship. But when you're no longer on top of your game and have become defenseless, needy and wounded with nothing left to give, the real heart motives of others become crystal clear.

Friends and Followers often offer you the same words when you crash and burn:

They love you. They're praying for you. They hope for your best.

But a friend takes caring one step further. It's a big one. They do something.

They refuse to allow you to throw in the towel. They remind you that you are far too valuable to the body of Christ to quit now. They will not let you go no matter what. They say, "I'm going to be there for you no matter what," or "I believe in you even when you don't, and I know you're going to make it!" They assist in the rescue, restoration and revival of your soul. They hold you when you weep and feel like you can't go another step. They call when no one else does just to see how you are, and they don't expect you to act holy when you're not. And when you think you've reached the end of your rope, they make a loop in the rope to attach to your wrist, so you can't simply lose your grip.

In the same way, Jesus is that kind of friend. He will never

leave you or forsake you regardless! As I said earlier—
He is unafraid to gently bandage your ghastly wounds
and to meet the desperate need of the moment, to heal
you wherever you are hurt. He's not afraid to get dirty or
risk associating with you when you're down and out. Our
God will stand with you through your brokenness or in
the awkward silence of the night season. He will love you
with each and every step you make toward wholeness. He
will silence your accusers while pouring into your wound
the healing oil of the Holy Spirit, giving you a brand new
start! So don't fixate on those who leave you, but embrace
a friend who sticks closer than a brother!

*I embrace your healing hands, oh, Jesus, with all my heart!
Thank you that your kindness and restorative power inspire
me today to be a true friend to the next untouchable but
precious one whom you bring my way.*

Wounds of a Friend

"Faithful are the wounds of a friend, but deceitful are the kisses of an enemy" (Prov. 27:6).

Dear Precious One,

Have you noticed that the older you get, the more you reflect on life and what it means? Many are careful to ponder things, learn from past mistakes, and see the positive in any situation ... and that's a good thing. But it is human nature to surround ourselves with people who tell us what we 'want to hear' rather than what we 'need to hear'. Let me add here that I can't help but notice that my greatest growth has come by not only listening to sound wisdom, but also to what was a hard word. Too often we discard wisdom from others because it hurts, and as a result we fail to benefit from it.

The people in my life who have helped me the most during the past few years are not the twenty cheerleaders who regularly cheer me on but rather the one or two who have a track record of wisdom and actually speak the truth without holding back. Initially, I am not attracted to those people. To be perfectly honest, I would much rather hang with those who make me feel good about myself. But when I humble myself and receive their wisdom I break old barriers and take new ground. Strongholds and mindsets are then broken and, as a result, I become more 'Christlike' and mature. It is then that I am better prepared for God to use me.

Over the years even my harshest critics—those who have caused severe pain—have helped me. The truth is My enemy can be my friend if I humble myself and ask God, "Is there any wisdom in what they are saying? Are you trying to work through them to change my character? If so, show me the truth and help me to be willing to learn from this experience." At that point I am open to the gentle revelations of the Holy Spirit, to transform my heart and change my character into the likeness of Christ.

We all have friends, but what really makes a good friend? All true friends share a common quality—they are not afraid to speak the truth or bring up an unpopular subject. Because of their boldness and willingness to share their hearts with me I have, more than once, been prevented from making a shipwreck of my life. They may not have always communicated things tactfully, but I knew they meant well and wanted God's best for me. How foolish I would've been had I walked away because their words made me uncomfortable. Today I have great respect for the wisdom that was birthed through the fire of a 'word in season'.

Today we live in a society that is passive and embraces

everyone and everything. Few today feel comfortable confronting someone. We would rather be liked and tell them what they want to hear to win their approval, but we must realize that real love speaks the truth even if it hurts, especially if prompted by the Holy Spirit. If you want to be liked by everyone sell ice cream, don't speak a word in season.

We are to "admonish one another with all wisdom." (Col. 3:16) In the *Dictionary of the New Testament* Colin Brown defines admonition: "To exert influence upon another (by life and word) to guide him/her into obedience of God's will as revealed in Scripture. It consists of reminding, warning, counseling, correcting, reproving, and rebuking a person with the intention that he/she will carry it out." Chip Ingram, President of Walk Thru the Bible, says, "Admonition is God's antibiotic for the church; done Biblically, it is the most loving thing you can do . . . for all concerned."

We are often blinded to our own faults, whether we pretend they are not there, don't see them at all, or are simply unwilling to come to terms with them. That's why God specifically places others in our lives to help us see the blind spots, so we can become all God intends us to be.

"Who can discern his errors?" asks David. **"Acquit me of hidden faults."** (Psalms 19:12, NASB) Building relationships with other wise Christians provides an opportunity for us to grow and exposes areas of sin or struggle while illuminating the blind spots we do not see. Habits, sin, and weaknesses can easily destroy our lives or place us on a road that may take years to recover from. True love will provide a safe place where we speak into each others' lives. What greater gift of love can we give? **"As iron sharpens iron, so one man sharpens another."** (Prov. 27:17)

Once I graduated from Bible College, my folks, who were Pastors, generously offered me the chance to speak nearly every other Sunday morning in my father's pulpit. At times I would preach a series of messages, three weeks in succession. Knowing this was a precious gift I did not take it lightly. Even today I can't get over such a rare act of kindness. Afterwards, Dad and Mom would take me aside to encourage me, telling me how proud they were. Then they would offer suggestions on how to improve.

I am so thankful that my parents were brutally honest with me and that I did not allow pride or an unteachable spirit to rob me of the precious gift of wisdom they gave me.

Because of those opportunities and their mentoring I was able to grow and improve my ministry. It wasn't always easy when they corrected me, but I knew that, more than anything, they loved me and wanted God's best for me. Looking back, I praise God that they cared enough to speak the truth even when it hurt. I would not be where I am today without my parents' wise input, and I honor them for their love and boldness in speaking into my life. It has always been my godly parents who were used most to bring healing and restoration into my life.

I believe that, often, mighty warriors abort their spiritual development when things get tough and uncomfortable, but those who persevere will become partakers with Christ in their holy calling. The deeper life requires humility, unusual obedience and a crucifixion of the flesh, but as we yield in this area we are resurrected through the power of the Holy Spirit into a deeper walk with Christ. And not only that but He knows He can trust us with more responsibility when the time comes, because we were obedient in the small things.

It is not always easy to speak truth into the life of someone you love. We worry about damaging the relationship, causing permanent wounds. We might even ask, "What if my friend misunderstands me and gets angry or hurt?" At that point we must pray for wisdom, asking God to speak through us. But regardless of the discomfort on both sides of a confrontation, if it is a spirit-led urge rather than a fleshly one, we dare not ignore God's command to confront, but we should also do it in love, encouraging our brothers toward greater depths of relationship with God. And no matter how painful confrontation is, its end result can be healing and wisdom if received in the right spirit. In fact, the Bible says, **"Faithful are the wounds of a friend, but deceitful are the kisses of an enemy."** (Prov. 27:6)

Speaking the truth in love doesn't mean we can't speak the hard truth or that we must hide the facts, or cover up sin. God uses difficult people to file down the rough spots in our flesh, rooting out blind spots and weaknesses. In truth we learn more from difficult people than from persons who have patted us on the back. It is not always easy to receive, and at times we even run from those people. In the end, however, it is clear that tough words were the means by which God transformed us.

"We are his workmanship," (Eph. 2:10) and God uses others, even our enemies to conform us into the image of our Lord. May we humble ourselves and receive these lessons, refusing to take another walk around Mt. Sinai until we learn our way. If we have teachable spirits we will, like joyful, obedient children, learn from whatever tutor our Father chooses, knowing we will ultimately bear the peaceful fruit of righteousness and reflect the character of our wonderful Lord.

Dear Precious Lord, I humble my heart before You. Make me soft and pliable, willing to listen to the wisdom of others. Use them to cut away my flesh and reveal my blind spots so I can grow and become all You want me to be. I am the clay in the Potter's hands ... mold me into a vessel of honor fit for your use. Thank You for always having my best interest at heart.

The Deeper Life

"Then Jesus said to his disciples, "Whoever wants to be my disciple must deny themselves and take up their cross and follow me." (Matthew 16:24, NIV)

Dear Precious One,

In every age there are a few that seem to break free from mediocrity and apathy. These hungry Trailblazers for God yield their lives to following hard after God. Their hearts yearn for something deeper and more meaningful than just a status quo relationship with the Savior.

We know that "wide is the road that leads to destruction and narrow is the way that leads to life." (Matthew 7:13) Hell's Highway is wide and broad with people standing shoulder to shoulder, toe to heel, slowly edging toward the clefts of destruction. There is also a narrow road that leads to life; if you were to sit under a tree and watch those that pass you by you would notice one person at a time pass every so often.

Child of God, there is also within the body of Christ a broader path called 'status quo', many of the body of Christ are on this road, they are saved and have heaven as their final destination, but are not seeking God's highest. There is also a narrow gate that leads us down a path far less traveled. On this path you will find many twists and turns with bumps and places where you must take that leap of faith to continue. This is the road called 'sacrifice'. With the sweat still on your brow you can walk this unpopular road. Not many want to.

Many traveling down the road called 'status quo' have become content with what they've always had. They are enamored by the 'blessings of God', they seek God for what He can do for them and they have become spiritually satisfied with His hands. They desire a life of ease, comfort, and simplicity. They don't want to hear about 'carrying a cross' or 'denying self'. It is far easier to seek after a basic mainstream message that makes one feel good and leaves one motivated.

Others who are traveling down the path called 'sacrifice' are not content with following a crowded highway everyone else seems to be on. They know that only His face will truly satisfy the deepest longing of their hearts, they realize He is worth pursuing! They have a kingdom mindset that sees things in the light of eternity and not the temporal here and now. They cry out with passion, "Jesus I want a deeper life only found in you."

What is the deeper life? The deeper life is walking on a road far less traveled where consecration, humility, intimacy, devotion, and sacrifice is treasured; where one would rather invest their life in being a 'God pleaser' rather than a 'man pleaser'; where the Lord will rule and reign in our hearts forever; where one realizes that crowns are not given away as souvenirs, you must earn them; where taking up the cross and following hard after God, although difficult, still continues to bring contentment to one's soul.

Do you wish to live a deeper life? Living a life of sacrifice and devotion is a virtue most pleasing to God's majesty. Living with anything less only leaves one feeling empty and void. It is not good enough for us to think ourselves devout because of the number of prayers that we offer. If we go home and are arrogant and use harmful words amongst our neighbors and family we are only deceiving ourselves. Spiritual maturity must be more than just a desire or intention, it must be walked out.

We often go through this life trying to fill our existence with empty things and shallow appetites while we gradually grow weaker and colder in our soul until finally we have had enough. A hunger from deep within is birthed and we rise up and say in a desperate tone, "I want a deeper life!"

Why does it take so long to discover our spiritual condition and seek after the cure? We need courage to face the truth that we often conceal. Our weakness can be revealed and an intense hunger with our heart will burst a fresh and intimate encounter into the presence of God. Do we need him? Do we desperately long to feel his touch and presence in our life? Do we need him to release a spiritual hunger and take us off the road of 'status quo'? Do we need his mercy to deliver us from the snare of satisfaction and the sin of complacency that we have surrendered to? Do we need him to open our eyes to the desperation that should be pursued and longed after?

Let me warn you, my friend, that the deeper life will offend men. It is inevitable that, the moment desperation is released, certain friends may show up with 'words of encouragement' designed to quench your fire and lessen the intense hunger that is being released. They do this to help you, but their help will lead you back through that narrow gate and onto status quo highway.

When you pursue the deeper life passionately enough you will offend some of those who are closest to you but God is not offended by the intense hunger in your heart! We must silence the conflicting voices around us that speak, the voices that urge us to settle for less than God's best. Are you determined enough to arrest God's attention? Are you tired of standing on status quo highway being a spectator Christian while the faithful Saints pass you by on that road of sacrifice? Get desperate enough today to arrest the attention of God.

Cry out with all your heart and settle it within that you will have a deeper life found in Christ Jesus; refuse to walk down status quo highway twiddling your thumbs and not living up to your full potential. Get an appetite for the deeper things of God, move beyond just the blessings that come from His hands and embrace His heart as a close friend.

A genuine deeper life rooted in Christ will cause one to

love God not only in 'word' but in 'deed'. Sweet Surrender is the lily of virtues, it causes an absolute resolution to place God as number one. It is hard to convince ourselves that carrying a cross can bring peace and contentment. Could not God make it easier for us to live the deeper life without making us carry a cross? Yes he could, for all things are possible with God. He is all-powerful but able as He may be to save us from the difficult path of 'sacrifice' He has not chosen to do it.

He is the sweet master and we only need to adore him on this narrow path without fully understanding it. By walking the path of 'sacrifice' we clearly see that we never could become mature without first becoming humble, teachable, unselfish, and becoming detached from our self life. Sacrifice destroys self-love and causes one to become dead to self. We are becoming a fully developed 'new man' found in Christ Jesus.

As we walk down the narrow path of sacrifice He accomplishes His grand design for our lives. We become reliant on Him and He frees us from self by revealing our weakness and corruptions by His personal dealings in our lives. An intense desperation is created by the emptiness of all things. We discover the door way to the deeper life by first being discontent with a shallow existence.

We would love to fully know Christ and His pure love without it costing us anything, but it is only excessive self-love that desires to become mature at such a cheap rate. His fatherly heart does not take joy in seeing us struggle but He fully knows that the road of sacrifice leads one to become steadfast and meek where our motives and intentions are purified and make us worthy of carrying his precious heart.

Take joy, dear precious one, at bearing the cross down the windy and narrow road of 'sacrifice' for your joy is set before you as you embark into a 'deeper life'. You have embarked on a quest, a journey of divine proportions. You determined in your heart that nothing is worth more than the joy of running after God and leaning on His breast. You enter heaven knowing him as close friend for He is altogether lovely and in His presence you discover healing and the fullness of Joy.

You are my sweet Master and I adore you on this narrow path I am on. I do not fully understand it but I will trust You as I walk the path of 'sacrifice'. I fully embrace a humble, unselfish, and detached self life. I desire the deeper things of God found only in Your presence.

A Teachable Spirit

"Integrity is the glue that holds our way of life together. We must constantly strive to keep our integrity intact. When wealth is lost, nothing is lost; when health is lost, something is lost; when character is lost, all is lost." (Billy Graham)

Dear Precious One,

There is a quality of spirit deep within the heart that desires a far deeper Christian life. This quality is worth more than great riches, than the rarest jewel, than the greatest talent. It is the quality of a teachable spirit.

Children of God who desire to go deeper are teachable. As we study the life of Abraham, we can plainly see why he was so blessed. More than anything else, he valued instruction and a willingness to keep the commandments of God. Such a desire is much more than just a willingness to listen. We become teachable when our desire to receive wisdom is greater than our desire for comfort.

Do we have a willingness to be instructed? Are we humble enough to receive wisdom from the Lord and from others? At times we all become unteachable and refuse sound advice. The harsh truth is that during those times we would prefer to change the rules rather than comply. But that never gets us to a place of blessing; rather it destroys our lives. Scripture says pride comes before a fall, and, in any case, it leaves us out on a limb, alone.

I can't help but think of Naaman who wanted to be healed from the leprosy that was destroying his flesh, yet he ran off in an angry rage when God's messenger told him to simply go wash seven times in the Jordan River. It was an awkward, seemingly absurd command that made no sense to his natural mind. Why should he go dip in a dirty river when there were rivers far superior to that one in his own land? But the river wasn't really the problem in his case. His pride wouldn't let him humble himself enough to obey and be healed. In the end, his leprosy was cured only when he listened to wisdom, changed his mind, humbled his heart, and was obedient to follow a simple but clear instruction from a godly and anointed man.

In the same way we must realize that the deeper Christian life requires us to crucify the flesh, humble ourselves, and obey when our reasoning says otherwise. It requires active pursuit in seeking, hearkening to, and studying the Scriptures. As we humble ourselves, we are then stripped of pride and our hearts become soft and teachable, yearning more for intimacy than for independence and our own agendas.

Becoming teachable is a process. Are we teachable? Are we learning? Do we have a burning desire to embrace character and integrity even if it hurts?

> **"Now therefore, listen to me, my children,
> for blessed are those who keep my ways."**
> (Proverbs 8:32)

God blesses those who draw near, listening to the still, small voice of the Holy Spirit. Often we ignore His voice, His warnings, and even His vivid red flags because we refuse to listen. If we are not listening, we are not learning, and if we are not learning, we are not growing. The cycle never stops, and the blessing will not come until we stop what we're doing and begin to watch, wait, listen, and obey.

In Proverbs 8:34-35, God instructs us **to watch, wait, and search** for Him. Notice that these are all action verbs that we should practice every day. In fact, we should be daily alert to things He wants to teach us. And more than just being aware, we should diligently seek wisdom and truth, for Scripture says that those who seek Him will find Him.

In Hosea 4:6 it says, **"My people are destroyed for lack of knowledge. Because you have rejected knowledge, I also will reject you for being priest for me; because you have forgotten the law of your God, I also will forget your children."** Listening is serious business to God! Scripture warns that, if we reject God's teaching and ignore wisdom, He will bar us from becoming priests, representatives of His kingdom. Personally, I would rather not be passed over when He needs a useful vessel. In fact, if for me to live is Christ, I will want nothing more than to be in the center of His will.

In Leviticus 26:23-24 it says, **"If after all of this punishment *you still do not listen to me*, but continue to defy me, then I will turn on you and punish you seven times harder than before."** (Today's English Version) The key phrase here is, "if you still do not listen to me."

Also notice Proverbs 8:32-36: **"Now therefore, *listen to me*, my children, for blessed are those who keep my ways. *Hear instruction* and be wise, and do not disdain it. Blessed is the man who *listens to me*, watching daily at my gates, waiting at the posts of my doors. For whoever finds me finds life, and obtains favor from the Lord; but he who sins against me wrongs his own soul; all those who hate me love death."**

Scripture emphasizes the importance of listening to God, even mentioning it three times in this short passage. In the same way, Ezekiel 3:7 refers to the people of Israel as **"hard, impudent, and stubborn."** And if, like Israel, we have developed a bad habit of not listening, this Scripture also applies directly to us. (See Galatians 6:16.)

A teacher who has invested much time in a particular student needs evidence that the student has truly learned from his wisdom—that the time spent was a good investment. In a spiritual sense the proof comes when a student's life is transformed to live so as to glorify God. Where he was once reckless and immature, he now displays maturity, self-control, and a teachable heart.

Do we really have a burning desire to be taught? Do we honor and respect wisdom from a **"multitude of counselors?"** (Proverbs 15:22) Are we diligently seeking God's best in our lives, refusing to compromise our integrity and character? Are we motivated to become wise and apply this wisdom to our lives? Are we paying close attention to our teachers and refusing to pass up opportunities to learn? Are we learning from our past mistakes, refusing to keep falling into the same traps? To fall into a pit is one thing, to stay in there is another.

If we find ourselves lacking the desire to learn from God and others, it is usually because we have lost our first love and need a fresh revelation of who He is and how much He loves us, along with a healthy dose of the fear of the Lord. Having a healthy fear of God is key: **"Who is the man that fears the Lord? Him shall he teach in the way he chooses"** (Psalms 25:12). Listen and learn from your past mistakes. Have a teachable spirit, and be that person of God.

You have called me for such a time as this! Let it be, oh God, according to your Word. Give me ears to hear sound wisdom and courage to live an obedient life. Mighty warriors who desire to go deeper are teachable.

Discipline

"For the LORD corrects those he loves, just as a father corrects a child in whom he delights." (Proverbs 3:12)

Dear Precious One,

Aren't we, as God's children, fortunate to have a Father who loves us enough to direct our paths with this tool called 'discipline'? It hurts an earthly father when his child pouts and rebels, but the father endures this because he loves his child. He could refuse to be that kind of father and instruct his children, or if he really wanted, he could ignore their needs altogether.

Our heavenly Father would never do that to us. He will always show us the path of righteousness rather than allowing us to wander down the dead-end streets of our own shortsighted choosing, no matter what it costs Him. Our understanding is limited and our choices are often foolish and futile. But as a loving Father, He will protect us from ourselves when we are disobedient, making smaller and smaller the box in which we live, limiting our choices. But if we're obedient we can count on Him to guide us, making sure that we don't take the wrong turn and wind up lost, frightened, and lonely.

It's difficult to recognize discipline as something that is done not only to correct sin and disobedience, but also to deal with our sinful nature so that we may be changed to reflect the character of Christ.

How could God possibly toughen the fibers of our being or mold us to make us strong and holy if everything comes to us easily? He uses discipline and correction to mold us into that magnificent finished product—the creative design He imagined before the beginning of time. But there is a cost. The cost will often be pain and discomfort in the learning process, but we need to allow discipline to do its work within us. Will you let God take the reins in your life? Will you give Him full control and trust His loving hand to make you a vessel of honor? Will you trust His loving discipline and bow to His will?

If you really want to be that kind of mighty warrior, God will need to set you straight at times. He will take you from where you are and cut away the dead branches in your life. It never feels good to be pruned, but we know our Father only does so out of His great love so that we will reflect the awesome glory of God!

Yes, God, take the reins in my life. I give you full control and trust your loving hand to make me a vessel of honor. I trust your loving discipline and bow to your will. I say YES to your leadership in my life.

Pure Abandon and Sweet Surrender

"Looking at the man, Jesus felt genuine love for him. "There is still one thing you haven't done," he told him. "Go and sell all your possessions and give the money to the poor, and you will have treasure in heaven. Then come, follow me."

"At this the man's face fell, and he went away sad, for he had many possessions." **(Mark 10:21-22)**

Dear Precious One,

What an incredibly heartbreaking story we see when we read about the rich young ruler! I have often spent time pondering how this story actually played out. I can imagine an excited young man who is eager to follow after Jesus. His excitement got the attention of the Savior when he asked how to inherit eternal life. Jesus responded by telling him to obey the commandments. The young man blurted out, "I've already done that!" So Jesus, who was both prophetic and intuitive, looked him straight in the eye and with tender love put his finger on the crux of the issue—what was really holding this young man back.

"There's one thing left: Go sell whatever you own and give it to the poor. All your wealth will then be heavenly wealth. And come follow me." (v. 21)

But at this, the young man looked down quickly, breaking the steady gaze of tender affection, probably wiping a tear from his cheek, and then slowly walked away from Jesus with a heavy heart. He was stunned and dismayed at what he would have to pay to follow Christ. The cost was far too high to even consider; how could he give up his wealth and security and follow Him with nothing but blind faith?

If you could actually see this story unfold, you would also notice the face of Jesus, disappointed and wounded. He was actually traded away for material wealth. No doubt His eyes welled with tears, revealing the bitter sting of rejection that choked Him. Scripture says He dearly loved the young man. This visual has forever been branded on my heart. I never want to cause my Lord that kind of pain by trading Him for something I would not surrender. I refuse to walk away from Him with my head bowed in shame. That mental picture alone has renewed my zeal to obey.

Whatever became of the rich young man? If he continued on the same course during his life I'm sure he lived to regret that day. Eventually he will look into the eyes of

Jesus again on Judgment Day, and no doubt he will weep bitter tears of regret, after trading eternity in heaven for material wealth. In the end, he will see that his wealth mattered little in light of eternity.

Dear Precious One, we have the blessed opportunity to abandon our personal agendas in sweet surrender to Christ. Now is the time to make Him number one. The Lord needs warriors who are willing to leave it all and allow Him complete control of our lives; this begins by handing over our rights and giving Him first place without resentment or regret, relinquishing the throne of our lives, and allowing Him to rule from that position of authority. In this way we become useful tools He can use in whatever way He sees fit. And once we do that, He can trust us with great blessings and responsibility. We don't have to understand it all, but we do have to choose to believe that He knows exactly what He's doing, and that the outcome will be glorious!

He knows what you need, and what you are most suited to do for Him. You must be in that place of complete faith, depending on Him alone. Once you're able to take that step, you'll be able to see and understand, with the eyes of heaven, the reason He has placed you where you are. Pure abandonment and sweet surrender are the key to spiritual growth, but it is not easy to accept His grace by forsaking your flesh and staying immovable in faith when things get tough.

What, exactly, is involved in pure abandonment and sweet surrender? To put it simply, it involves giving up all your concerns and putting them in God's hands, forgetting about yourself and concentrating only on Him. Abandonment means we choose not to interfere in the process when God is transforming us to the image of Jesus Christ. When this is true of us, we will embrace His will no matter how much it hurts, yielding ourselves to His intentions in all things. When we can do that, it will bring about an absolute declaration of His purpose in our lives. And in the process we will become those Mighty Warriors He designed us to be.

Some people say that they will only abandon self when they understand God's ways. The problem with such a notion is that we'll never be able to understand God's ways to that extent. We'll never understand His reasoning. We can't even begin to conceive the knowledge and wisdom of God or His intentions. That's where faith comes in. We can't fret. We must trust, because God loves us unconditionally, with a love that never ends. And He will always be faithful if we can just trust His integrity.

Through abandonment, the Lord is ultimately able to offer us the greatest possible display of His love and provision. In the process He will bring us to a place of maturity and knowledge that we love Him above all else, and that we're trustworthy with great things. What more could a person want?

Help me, oh Lord, to abandon my personal agenda in sweet surrender to you. Now is the time to make you number one. I desire to leave it all and allow you to have complete control of my life. I hand over my rights and give you first place. I relinquish the throne of my life, and allow you to rule and reign. I submit to your leadership.

His Hair Began to Grow Again...

"Then the Philistines seized him and gouged out his eyes; and they brought him down to Gaza and bound him with bronze chains, and he was a grinder in the prison. 22However, the hair of his head began to grow again after it was shaved off. 25It so happened when they were in high spirits, that they said, "Call for Samson, that he may amuse us." So they called for Samson from the prison, and he entertained them. And they made him stand between the pillars..."
(Judges 16:21-22,25)

Dear Precious One,

Consider the heartbreaking story of Samson who traded the secret of his anointed strength for sin. How foolish he was to throw away his supernatural power in his lust for a traitorous, immoral woman. Yet he did, and he suffered greatly for it.

When he revealed to her the secret of his incredible physical strength—his hair that had never been cut since birth, she shaved it off, leaving him powerless against his captors.

At that time, mortal enemies would punish captives by brutally gouging out their eyes, thus rendering them harmless. Once Samson was taken captive, they gouged out his eyes and bound him in chains, forcing him to grind grain for hours every day, tied to a massive millstone, as if he were little more than an ox. As awful as this was, as is often the case, the punishment was unavoidable. He turned away from God when he looked at and lusted after what God had forbidden. Humiliated and alone, he had time to realize that he had brought his grievous suffering on himself. He knew but ignored the truth, that if God's people fail to keep their focus on God alone and turn away from temptation, they will fall into enemy hands and lose their anointing—their usefulness to God.

Though sightless, his spiritual vision was suddenly sharp, and he realized he was powerless without the Lord. Then came the day when his enemies arranged a celebration and said, "Call for Samson, that he may amuse us!" In front of 3,000 Philistines, he was ruthlessly ridiculed and mocked, yet Samson called out to God, and the strength that he had lost by sin he recovered by prayer!

The hair of his head had begun to grow again. Did you catch that? His hair was growing! All that was lost was recovered! Our God is the God of recovery and restoration! Great were the misdeeds of Samson, and he paid a terrible price for his sin, but he found mercy when he once again cried out to God. He repented and God forgave him. In fact, the celebration ended abruptly when Samson pulled down the pillars that held up the building, killing every one of the Philistines. Remarkably, he is listed in the Hall of Faith in Hebrews 11, honored alongside Gideon, David, and Samuel. In the last moments of his life, Samson returned to God, and God answered his prayer and used him greatly.

Perhaps you've become spiritually blind due to lust of the flesh. You have looked at evil things and this has led to blurred spiritual vision, chains that bind you, grinding in a prison where you do not belong. Maybe you even traded your birthright for a cheap bowl of soup. Not only have you lost your eyes (spiritual vision) but you have lost your hair (glory and anointing) as well as your good name and reputation. The enemy has made you a laughing stock to the underworld. You are despised and rejected by men and now you bow your head in shame, wondering if God could ever restore you. If that describes you, I want you to know that God loves to give restoration and second chances to those who repent.

Cry out to Him with all your heart and soul, humbly repent for trading your anointing for sin. He will hear your cry for help and answer you. He will give you new vision to see things from His perspective. He will destroy the chains that bind you, and you will walk out of that prison and into your destiny. God declares you righteous because of the blood of Jesus, and says you will recover all! Trust Him, and know He will rescue and restore you. He will revive you, and you will reclaim all, for He is your refuge and strength, and by His power your hair will grow again!

You are a God of recovery and restoration! You love to give second chances to those who truly repent. You will revive me, and I will reclaim all, for you are my refuge and strength, and by your power my hair will grow again!

R Henra
wone

Chesvan 19
5783

Recover all!

In Jesus

11/13/2022

The Seed

"The seed that fell on the footpath represents those who hear the message, only to have Satan come at once and take it away." (Mark 4:15)

Dear Precious One,

2 Corinthians 2:11 tells us: **"...so that Satan will not outsmart us. For we are familiar with his evil schemes."**

Satan has had thousands of years to sharpen his skills in ripping off God's people. How does he do it? He creates an evil scheme to rob us of the divine seeds that our precious Holy Spirit has planted in our hearts. These seeds are the very words of God. His Word is His power, His life, and His very DNA.

"For the word of God is alive and powerful. It is sharper than the sharpest two-edged sword." These seeds (the Word of God) give us an advantage over the evil one; they are our weapon of choice.

Ever since the garden, that slithery snake has tried to get man to doubt the Word of God. "Did God really say?" If he can inject doubt, he can steal your seed. Just read about Adam and Eve, Moses, and Abraham, for instance, and you'll see how the human race has repeatedly fallen for the devil's lies. And he's still doing the same things today. At every opportunity he twists God's promises and makes us wonder about His commitment to us. *Is He really trustworthy? What will happen when my job ends?* And on and on it goes.

Child of God, stop allowing the enemy to rob you of your seed! If he can steal your seed, he can disarm you of your weapon and rob you of your potential, rendering you harmless against the kingdom of darkness when God meant you to be a mighty warrior. He desires to leave you a wounded warrior, cut down to size, full of worries and uncertainty, and doubting that God still speaks today.

Have you ever received a personal truth of who He is? Have you ever lain in His presence, resting in His delight? Then do not be unaware of your enemy who desires to steal that personal revelation of who your Jesus is! He comes after the seeds (the Word of God) that have been sown in your heart, trying his best to snatch them away from you. Don't let him!

Satan replaces the seeds of God with his own deadly seeds of doubt, fear, and confusion. He leaves his victims wounded and empty. But God has another plan! His plan is to cause the holy seeds that have been imparted to your heart to come out of your mouth! His Word on your lips brings power and victory. When Jesus confronted the devil with the Word, "It is written," Satan was defeated.

In the same way you will defeat the enemy when you speak out the very Word of God! God declares over you today:

"He made my mouth like a sharpened sword, in the shadow of his hand he hid me; he made me into a polished arrow and concealed me in his quiver." (Isaiah 49:2)

Within your heart is His Word: **"Is not my word like a fire, declares the LORD, and like a hammer that breaks a rock in pieces?"** (Jeremiah 23:29) So take the **"helmet of salvation and the sword of the Spirit, which is the word of God"** (Eph. 6:17) to protect your seed and guard your life from every trap of the enemy. I declare you shall be a Child of Honor, standing strong against the trickery of the evil one. And remember this: there are times when you have thoughts that cause you to lose hope that you will ever be a godly man, but consider the source: those thoughts do not originate with you, but are planted by your enemy!

You are a brand new creation with the mind of Christ once you accept His gift of salvation. God has equipped you to use His authority and tell the enemy to leave, in Jesus' name! When you use that authority, you render him harmless, so that he flees in terror when he hears the mighty name of Jesus coming out of your mouth. Once you get that profound truth deep in your spirit, you will no longer be easily deceived or robbed of your seed, so take up your armor, and fight to win!

Father God, place the fire of your Word in my heart that I may stand strong against the traps of the enemy! Protect my seed.

Do you Dream of Success or Worry about Failure?

"As he thinketh in his heart, so is he..."
(Prov. 23:7, KJV)

Dear Precious One,

There are those of us who tend to focus on past mistakes while others can't wait to move ahead and give it another try! Failure can leave us crippled, stuck in the past, and ultimately rob us of our God-given destiny to create the life of our dreams. Failure, in and of itself, does not have to be final. From God's point of view, the ultimate failure occurs only when we fail to pick ourselves up and try again to meet our true potential.

The Book of Proverbs tells us that the way we think determines who we are:

"As he thinketh in his heart, so is he..." (Prov. 23:7)

In other words, every time we fixate on negative thoughts of failure, that is exactly what we're going to get, because like attracts like. So fixating on failure will only cause us to lose our self-confidence and our ability to focus, which then inhibits our ability to succeed.

There once was a man named Karl Wallenda, a high-wire trapeze artist who was famous for his death-defying feats. At age seventy-three, Wallenda plummeted to his death while attempting to walk a tightrope strung several stories in the air between two skyscrapers in San Juan, Puerto Rico.

In comparison to many of his previous heart-stopping acrobatic feats, walking a tightrope was rather mundane. He had successfully walked tightropes thousands of times in the past. But three months prior to the event something changed and he began to experience severe anxiety and a fear of falling.

A rather intuitive reporter wrote an article at the time of his death, which included this statement:

"When Karl Wallenda poured his energies into not falling, rather than into walking the tightrope, he was destined to fall."

Karl had been the creator of his own destiny. His fixation on failure was manifested in his mind's eye and came to life in his catastrophic fall. Like Wallenda, our chances of failure are increased tenfold when we fixate on the negative. Like attracts like, whether good or bad. What we sow ... we reap.

But there are many who use their apprehension in a

very different way. When used to its greatest advantage, apprehension can actually drive us to achieve great things. Rather than allowing apprehension to paralyze us or to be a negative mental force, apprehension can create excitement and a feeling of adventure to prove the naysayer (in us) wrong and encourage us to go higher than ever before. Apprehension knocked on the door; faith opened it and nothing was there.

If you have given up on a previous dream due to failure, Scripture says it's time to stand up, dust yourself off, and try again!

"...Plans to prosper you and not to harm you, plans to give you hope and a future." (Jeremiah 29:11)

The Lord doesn't want you to give up. He wants you to break out of the cycle of self-doubt and fear. He wants to empower you to achieve your dreams.

But sometimes God wants us to take the first step. Ignore those little voices in your head and those around you who try to steal your self-confidence. Take the first step, and God will be with you, rooting for you on the rest of the way!

It also helps to look at the situation from a different perspective. Refuse to look at failure and past mistakes as forever missed opportunities and ultimate defeat, instead, choose to embrace your failures as new ways to learn and strengthen your individual God-given abilities. Thomas A. Edison's experiments failed many times before he finally found success. In fact, he once made this incredibly encouraging statement: "I have not failed. I've just found 10000 ways that won't work." He had the right idea, looking at every unsuccessful experiment as a way to eliminate one more equation that didn't work, in order to find the one that did.

The only thing worse than failing, is not trying at all. Learning from our mistakes teaches us how to be better, faster, and stronger the next time. Don't deny or hide from your mistakes. Embrace them. Learn from them. Improve and grow from them and don't make the same mistake again!

You have a choice: you can listen to negative self-talk and to the naysayers in your life or you can believe what God has promised us all along—that we are to enjoy our lives, that we can achieve anything under the heavens through Christ, because not only is He with us, He's in us.

You only live once, so make it count. Make God proud! Get up again and try again, Mighty Child of God!

"You can do all things through Christ who gives you strength!" (Philippians 4:13)

The crowds of heaven are cheering you on—so what are you waiting for? Go turn the world upside down for Jesus! Dear Lord, I lean on you and trust in the power of the Holy Spirit to see this come to pass.

Dark Night of the Soul

*"By night on my bed I sought him whom my soul
loveth: I sought him, but I found him not."
(Song of Solomon 3:1)*

Dear Precious One,

The Shulamite girl of the Song of Solomon found herself in
a season of darkness, pursuing her Lover, but couldn't find
Him. A deep yearning caused her to rise up and pursue
the object of her affection.

**"I will rise now, and go about the city in the streets,
and in the broad ways I will seek him whom my soul
loveth: I sought him, but I found him not."** (v.2)

As darkness began to fall, she grew increasingly desperate
to find her one true love, but her search was in vain.

Alone and anxious, she felt abandoned and afraid, unable
to sense His presence anywhere. I can see her face—her
eyes dark and distant, feeling terribly lost and confused.
She walked all alone with no one to comfort her, until she
reached out to a watchman and cried out in desperation:

"Have you seen the one my heart loves?" (v.3) With no response, she turned away. Disappointed, she walked on alone.

All at once, in the darkness of the night she discovered Him!

"Scarcely had I passed them when I found the one my heart loves. I held him and would not let him go." (v.4)

She embraced Him and refused to let go! The yearning and desire did a deep work inside her. She could now rest, reunited with the one who was **"altogether lovely."** (SOS. 5:16) Through a dark night she discovered a deep longing that could only be satisfied by finding Him.

Mighty warrior, at some point you too will face a dark night when it seems that all is lost, and your spiritual vision has become blurred—when you can't sense the nearness of His presence or reach out and touch Him. You feel like asking, "Where has He gone?" The sense of abandonment is palpable, and God feels a million miles away. Perhaps you're in that battle now.

You reach out to others, but they don't understand you, nor can they help you. All at once you discover inside a deep desperation that you didn't know existed. It propels you from that place of spiritual apathy into a full-blown pursuit of God. Your spiritual hunger begins to grow within you.

It might help to know that there's a purpose to the dark night of the soul—because we feel alone, anxious and desperately needy, we are especially motivated to seek God earnestly. If we understood what was going on, we would actually short-circuit the process. It's the not knowing that creates a yearning for God, motivating us to rise up to pursue Him. We must permit it to run its course and accomplish God's objectives in our lives.

Darkness always vanishes with the sunrise. And with it comes hope; you're facing a brand new season. With this new day comes the revelation that you were never alone, even in the darkness of the night. His presence was still there with you, yet it was hidden so that you would desire Him and pursue Him above all else. Do you love Him most?

Before apathy falls away we experience heartache and pain in our desperate search. Self is set aside when we realize our desire for God can be satisfied only by God Himself. Everything else fades in importance compared to being in His presence during the dark night of the soul.

If you're in a dark season, it's time to rise up, Mighty Warrior, and pursue the object of your affection! Wait on the Lord and refuse to go by your feelings; just know that morning is coming when you will soar high on wings like eagles. You will run and not grow weary. You will walk and not faint!

"Dark night of the soul" sounds like a threatening and much to be avoided experience. If we in no way experience the chill of a dark and cold winter, it is very unlikely that we will ever cherish the warmth of a brilliant summer's day. In the

dark night we learn to *beseech God, with great yearnings, as He takes from us our imperfections and faults. Even so, Lord, let it be!*

Fierce Determination

*"He gives power to the faint, and to him who has no
might he increases strength. Even youths shall faint
and be weary, and young men shall fall exhausted; but
they who wait for the Lord shall renew their strength;
they shall mount up with wings like eagles; they shall
run and not be weary; they shall walk and not faint."
(Isaiah 40:29-31)*

Dear Precious One,

We live in the age of ease where many want to take the
path of least resistance. Why? Because who in the world
wants to struggle? Struggle is uncomfortable. Everywhere
we turn we're told to "Pamper yourself. You deserve it" or
to "Take the easy way."

The problem with this approach is that it creates a
mentality that says, "Everything should come quickly
and effortlessly." We'd much prefer to go through life
with the same mindset: no resistance, no battles, and no
trials. We have it all wrong: struggle is what builds fierce
determination into our character. It is in the wilderness

experience that we learn this first hand.

Let me illustrate: a baby eaglet is hatched when it uses its tiny custom-designed egg-tooth to peck away at the eggshell. It's the fierce determination and struggle of the eaglet that ultimately brings him out of captivity. He pecks and pecks at that shell until he finally breaks through. If you were to watch this arduous process, you would want to help the baby eaglet out. It feels like we're being mean sitting by and doing nothing to help the little guy while he struggles!

In reality, however, it would be a tragedy if you broke the shell to set the baby bird free. It's only during the process of 'struggling' that the eaglet learns determination and builds physical strength and stamina that will preserve his very life. When the eagle is older, he'll have to take hold of his prey and never let go. In fact, he would die if he did.

Most of the eagle's strength is in his talons, which must grip his prey no matter what. When the little bird reaches maturity, he'll become one of the most ferocious warriors in the animal kingdom. A raptor's talons must be strong, but his mindset must be even stronger. The eagle must chase his prey until it becomes exhausted and then zoom down upon it at speeds exceeding 100 MPH; this tenacity is born as the eagle strives to break out of his shell.

Like all predators, that eagle will experience far more failures than successes. If he became easily discouraged, his size, strength, and powers of flight and vision would be of little use to him. If he were to let go of his prey when the struggle became agonizing, he wouldn't have long to live.

Fierce determination is born of struggle for humans as well as eagles. Sometimes struggles are exactly what we need in our lives. If God allowed us to go through our lives without any obstacles, it would cripple us. We would never be as strong as we could have been. And we certainly would never soar!

Remember... What we struggle with makes us strong!

The common misconception of many of today's Christians is that God is blind to their struggles, only blesses other people, and excludes them, forcing them to do things the hard way. This lie of Satan exists to muddy the vision God has created regarding struggles that, in the end, actually empower us. Unfortunately, many wounded warriors lay on the battlefield defeated because of this deadly and erroneous mindset. Before we can grasp the true value of the struggle, we must learn to rest in His unfailing love, refusing to doubt that love. If we allow Satan to twist our view of God's love, then he will succeed in giving us a warped mentality about the benefits of the struggle.

It's difficult to grasp the overwhelming love of God. We can begin to understand it by getting to know His precious Son, Jesus Christ. God's love never fails and doesn't change; He knows us intimately, and yet He still loves us, in all our weaknesses. The children of Israel turned against God time and time again. It boggles the mind to realize that He constantly turned His love toward them even after they worshiped other gods. His love and mercy are so awesome that they are inconceivable to comprehend with our limited human intellect. We must realize that the very essence of His nature is to discipline us and to love us back to health.

Accepting God's love means not only believing that He loves us, but also trusting Him enough to place our very lives in His hands, knowing His plans are only good, and will benefit us in the end. When we can finally rest in Him we will begin to live in unity with Him so He can trust us with His plans and secrets, as well as His deepest desires. What better place can we be than where He can share the treasures of His very heart? With this new knowledge, I pray that you'll look differently at struggles and see them as a training ground for greatness...

Lord, I know I will face struggles in this life so hold me close and give me the fierce determination to run my race no matter what season I am in! Make me strong!

Jumping for Joy

"Praise be to the Lord, for he has heard my cry for mercy. The Lord is my strength and my shield; my heart trusts in him, and I am helped. My heart leaps for joy and I will give thanks to him in song."
(Psalm 28:6, 7)

Dear Precious One,

When was the last time that you prayed with excitement and joy?

In the story of David, our hero was facing insurmountable odds. Just when it seemed as if everyone and everything was working against him to destroy him, David prayed.

David prayed for deliverance from his enemies. But he did much more than simply send up a quick prayer. He pleaded for God to listen to him, to hear him, and ultimately to save him.

Read those verses again. David was so certain that God would come to his rescue that he was simply overjoyed, knowing that he had someone to approach for help, to *hear* him. At that time God hadn't even answered his prayer or delivered David and his people from the evil they were facing, but David was simply too overjoyed to care.

He already knew that God would come to his aid. He was that certain. David was overwhelmed with thanksgiving, realizing that the Holy Spirit encouraged him to ask God for help! He was already jumping for joy, bathed in relief after simply asking God to move. He already knew that his troubles were over because He was absolutely certain that God would protect him.

When was the last time you offered up such an exuberant and joyful prayer to God? When was the last time you prayed, convinced without a doubt that your prayer would be answered? When was the last time you prayed without doubt that God would intervene on your behalf? Why not begin doing it now?

Next time you offer one of your heaviest burdens to God to resolve in prayer, try jumping to your feet with lots of enthusiasm and energy. Then say these words,

"Thank You, God! I'm overwhelmed with gratitude that You reminded me to call on You! Whew! That's a load off my mind! It's all yours. I know You've got this under control, so I trust You to take over and do whatever You think is best!" Once you've done that, you can be confident and rest, knowing the end of the story will be glorious!

This is exactly what we mean by the incredible phrase my Grandpa Yost Byler always said, "Let go, and let God!"

Steve Porter

I give you my heaviest burdens, Lord, I lay them at your feet one by one. I will jump for joy with lots of enthusiasm and energy and give you my highest praise!

Arrows of God

"He has hidden me in the shadow of his hand. I am like a sharp arrow in his quiver." (Isaiah 49:2b)

Dear Precious One,

Jesus is looking for a Bride willing to be transformed into a 'vessel of honor' fit for His use. This transformation takes place in the lives of believers who proactively submit to the will of God. This process includes actions or behavior changes that prepare people for the work God has called them to do. It is never easy work, rather it is the 'molding' and 'shaping' through our obedience that transforms us into vessels that bring honor. We are His workmanship.

 The Lord's desire is to find a mature person of God who has done what is necessary to make himself ready for battle, one who has prepared himself. Of his own free will he has made that choice out of reckless abandon for his Father. This time is especially designed to equip and prepare us for the days ahead. God is now offering us an opportunity to prepare for eternity in His kingdom, but it is our choice whether or not we will prepare.

We may wonder if preparation is even possible, and if so, what that process entails. Adequate preparation is only possible with the help of the Holy Spirit; His training is not easy and requires effort on the part of each individual. Spiritual maturity does not come through a prayer line and is not imparted, but is walked out in the life of each individual.

Let's learn some lessons by looking closely at the arrow-making process:

A piece of wood went through a long and complex manufacturing process before it became a polished arrow in the hands of an Old Testament archer. It didn't happen overnight, the metal arrow head had to be hardened, tempered in fire. Much like an arrow, God's people must also go through the proverbial fire if they are going to be used by God to hit their target, living out their destiny. Hebrews 12:29 says, **"For our God is a consuming fire."** He purges us through the fire. A heart purged with fire is a heart captivated by His love. As the impurities surface His likeness is reflected inside us. When we deal with those impurities we grow to be like Jesus.

The process of arrow-making involves great patience. High quality, dependable arrows cannot be made in haste. Skilled Old Testament archers actually began making their arrows a year in advance. They first had to find just the right kind of wood, most often the branches of an almond tree, because its branches grew straighter than any other and it was one of the first to bud in spring. For our purposes the almond tree symbolizes 'resurrection power'.

God takes time and great patience to develop us into vessels of honor. As the fire burns away the dross (sin) in our lives, our obedience produces resurrection power (like the almond tree) that burns away the old things, and we become brand new creatures in Christ. We become those mighty warriors He designed us to be!

Once the branch was cut down the next step was to strip off the bark. Dead bark represents the removal of the flesh. Maturity takes time. Once He cuts the knots (strongholds) and burrs (bad habits) from our lives we become the type of arrow God can use. 'Stripping' is never comfortable but is a part of the process. Joseph was stripped of his coat of many colors (favor) before he finally put on the garments of a prime minister. He endured a long and painful stripping process before he eventually assumed his place of honor and authority (polished arrow).

"Your Lord desires to purify your soul, and He can use a very rough file. Yes, He may even assault the purer and nobler things of your life! These assaults serve as a revelation to awaken the human soul...for the soul to truly discover, to truly know, just how miserable is its natural state."

Michael Molinos

Archers would initially begin to shape the wood by sanding it. In the same way, friction (sanding) will bring you closer to Him if you let it. I want to encourage you not to become discouraged or disillusioned during the sanding process, because He is making the (Is. 45:2) **"crooked places straight"** (removing the knots and burrs). Next, the arrow is soaked in water to expose the grain of the wood. Just when we think we're ready to be used by God for our target (purpose) He lets us soak in the water of the Spirit. This brings to the surface the inner workings, thoughts, and imaginations of the heart that must be dealt with if we want to be vessels of honor.

More sanding and more soaking follows until the arrow is exactly the right size and shape. Though it may seem that such repetition is excessive, it's absolutely necessary for the production of high quality arrows. The Word of God sands flat the ungodly things in our lives. This, of course, is not enjoyable because we are not being used for our purpose yet, but without it we would fail to fly straight and hit our target with precision. Skipping steps and cutting corners will lead to inferior quality arrows that are incapable of serving the purpose for which they were created. This is why character development is so important if we want to make the grade as top-of-the-line arrows for the Kingdom of God.

At that point the archer places the arrow shaft in his quiver for a prescribed period of time. This is a proving time—the waiting room—that will prove whether the arrow will bow or warp. Before the archer can add the arrowhead to the shaft he must make sure the new shaft will stay straight. Shortchanging the arrow's proving time often means it will not make the grade. The quiver can be a very dark and lonely place, where we are frustrated and feel that little is being accomplished. But our heavenly Father knows best, and if we're not ready to be used we will begin our journey prematurely and miss our target entirely, resulting in great frustration and even causing us to question the call of God on our lives.

If you stay in the waiting room of the quiver until the archer takes you out, you will be proven strong and precise, ready to prove your worth. The archer will then select the bow and release you to hit your target and accomplish what He's called you to do.

We are God's arrows. He's the master archer, and our target is our purpose and destiny in life. He decides when to release us, sending us out toward that destiny. In His perfect timing He launches us to hit the target for greatest impact. It's not easy to go through fire, stripping, sanding, and soaking, but they are part of the process of becoming vessels of honor fit for His use. We are His workmanship and our obedience brings Him honor. You may feel like a wounded warrior when you're going through the process to be that vessel of Honor, but hold your course, because God is getting ready to use even the fire of affliction to propel you into your unique destiny!

I am your arrow oh God, prepare me no matter how difficult the process that I may hit my target in this life. Make me that vessel of honor fit for your use.

11/8/2022

re confirmed 4/27/2023 (Iyyar 6, 5783 ✡)

101

Humility

"A man's pride will bring him low, But a humble spirit will obtain honor." (Proverbs 29:23)

Dear Precious One,

Today we live in a world where few are interested in learning from others and where many would rather staunchly defend their positions than admit they're wrong. But God is raising up a generation marked by humility, who would rather learn from others than fall flat on their faces because of pride. Only those with humble, teachable spirits are privileged to walk in true purity of power, moving in the spirit and doing greater things than Jesus did. And you might have noticed that when such people stop listening and become impressed with themselves and what they know, God leaves to find another humble, useful vessel.

Dear Precious One, nothing expresses the character of Jesus the same way a meek and humble spirit does. We can live in peace knowing there's nothing standing between us and God. Our hearts are right with Him and our spirits are open to His leadership. We can be confident that when He speaks we will hear Him, and not be in confusion when trouble comes. Rather, we'll feel the beat of His heart and know the way we should go as we rest in His manifest presence, letting nothing distract us from the goal of glorifying God.

There is an old story about a student who went to a master and asked him to teach him. The master invited the student to sit with him and have tea. While they were seated, the master started to talk with the eager young student, but every time the master began to explain a point, the student would interrupt him and say, "Oh, I know that. I do this when that happens," or "I don't have that problem because. . . " Soon the master stopped talking and picked up the teapot. He began pouring tea into the student's cup. As the cup filled, he continued pouring until the cup overflowed and spilled out. The student shouted, "Stop! That's enough! My cup is full!" With that, the old master smiled and replied, "Yes, your cup is full, therefore I can teach you nothing until you empty your cup."

As humbling as it is to admit, I've had to learn these lessons the hard way. In fact, I've walked around that mountain more than once. But the older I get, the more I value sound wisdom from those who I know love me and have my best interests at heart. Walking in humility, knowing God intimately and feeling the beat of His heart causes me to trust that His words are life, health, and peace.

Mighty Warrior, in this day when God is searching the world over for those who will sit at His feet and listen, will

He find you available? May it ever be so, because He has incredible plans for those who have no agenda but His.

As time draws to a close we must carefully examine our hearts to see if we're in that teachable place, because only at His feet will we discover treasures found nowhere else on Earth.

Lord, help me to walk in humility, knowing you intimately and feeling the beat of your heart! May my heart remain right with you and my spirit open to your leadership. *Give me a teachable heart!*

Midnight Resolve

"So I went to Jerusalem and was there three days.
Then I arose in the night, I and a few men with me.
And I told no one what my God had put into my heart
to do for Jerusalem. There was no animal with me
but the one on which I rode. I went out by night by
the Valley Gate to the Dragon Spring and to the Dung
Gate, and I inspected the walls of Jerusalem that were
broken down and its gates that had been destroyed by
fire." (Nehemiah 2:11-13, ESV)

Dear Precious One,

Some leaders might have made a big deal of their entrance into the city of Jerusalem, but not Nehemiah! He entered three days before anyone realized it, and did a midnight assessment of the city's condition. No doubt he carefully inspected the damage and destruction while telling no one of the plans God gave him. He made his way through the city with a humble, quiet midnight resolve.

In v. 13, the word **'inspected'**, in Hebrew, is a medical term that means to probe a wound to determine the extent of an injury. Nehemiah carried a tremendous yearning for the restoration of Jerusalem, so he needed to understand the extent of the damage. His heart broke, seeing the city walls destroyed and the gates still smoldering. All appeared lost.

All was not lost, however! God raised up Nehemiah to bring healing to the city. Both vision and resolve had been laid on his heart, a resolve that burned in every fiber of his being. This godly man carried in him a holy, healing anointing that compelled him to act, and although he informed no one about inspecting the city, resurrection power was on the way. The plan and strategy had already been birthed, and within an astounding fifty-two days the walls were rebuilt, and Jerusalem was completely restored—in record time!

In the same way, God is raising up leaders who carry a quiet but powerful resolve for the rebuilding of righteousness in their communities—a burden that keeps them up at night. Heavenly plans for restoration have been downloaded into their hearts. God is the only one responsible for birthing a plan to bring new hope and healing to a city. This burden is so powerful that it propels them into the streets to inspect the damaged spiritual walls of their region. They walk with tears in their eyes, their hearts full of love and tender compassion. What are the strongholds that keep it captive, its prevailing wounds and greatest needs? Where does He want us to begin rebuilding? With these questions upmost in their minds they take their requests to God in intercession and fasting, and God gives them a plan of restoration to rebuild the lives of broken people.

Child of God, perhaps you feel wounded and broken, like damaged goods, but if that's true, this is your hour. Not only will God heal all your wounds and rebuild your walls, He desires to turn your test into a testimony and your mess into a message that will transform your little corner of the world as you allow the Holy Spirit to use you. He will give you a 'midnight resolve' that will rebuild the lives of broken people. Yes, God wants to use you (even the mistakes you may have made) to bring healing into the lives of others. He is looking for a Nehemiah who will answer the call to change the world for Jesus. Are you that person?

As I intercede and fast, download me with your plans of restoration to rebuild the lives of broken people in my region. Raise me up to carry that quiet but powerful resolve for the rebuilding of the walls of righteousness in my day.

The Cry for Spiritual Mothers and Fathers

"Even if you had ten thousand guardians in Christ, you do not have many fathers, for in Christ Jesus I became your father through the gospel." (1 Corinthians 4:15)

Dear Precious One,

Many people in the church have broken lives and have experienced more rejection and pain than most of us can even imagine. These struggling warriors aren't limited in age; they come from all walks of life, and they're desperate for a nurturing spiritual parent, someone to really care and help them find their identity and victory in Christ. Many are filled with self-doubt, fear, and even shame over the things that haunt their past. They want to bask in the warm glow of God's love, but they feel unworthy. Who will help them?

We should not be afraid to offer the encouragement, love, and support they so desperately need as surrogate spiritual mothers or fathers. In fact, our greatest joy comes when we lift up the fallen, encourage the brokenhearted, and touch others the way Jesus would—we are to be Jesus with skin on, to the world in which we live. That's the reason we're here!

Remember, Jesus himself acted as a spiritual Father to the fallen woman, a young lady with a sinful past. He did not throw stones and condemn her because, in His great love, He wanted to restore her. The Bible is filled with numerous examples of good people who temporarily lost their way but were eventually restored to God—people like Peter and King David, for example.

Many of today's lost children of God feel certain that He could never forgive what they've done. As a result, they walk away from the church and the Lord, feeling unworthy to seek help though they're desperate for it. And believe it or not, some are rejected by church people once they actually muster the courage to return to seek forgiveness.

This is an untenable situation—one God hates. In fact, right now He wants to raise up spiritual mothers and fathers to mentor the broken and lost, to bring healing and hope, to touch, heal and mature them. Our assignment is to refuse to give up on them or let them go until they're whole. This new breed of spiritual parents believes that each and every child of God is far too valuable to the body of Christ to condemn or throw away.

In 1 Corinthians 4:15 Paul himself said this: **"...that there were many guardians of Christ but not many fathers."** Even after 2000 years, we are still severely lacking in true spiritual mothers and fathers in the church today. Where are they?

It's not hard to minister to these precious wounded warriors. In fact, they eagerly soak up all the love, grace, kindness, gentleness, patience, encouragement, compassion, guidance and forgiveness we can give.

Jesus Christ was the ultimate spiritual Father. He possessed all of these qualities, and, on some level, we all do. After all, we are created in His image. True spiritual parents will lay down their lives for their children, are always willing to help build a child's character and resolve, ready to nurture the special gifts and qualities that others fail to see. Spiritual parents encourage these wounded warriors to make good use of their God-given gifts, and very often show them how. Today God is not only raising up pastors who have true shepherds' hearts, He also wants everyone in the body of Christ to mentor someone else. That's what community should be about.

A spiritual parent has a genuine Christ-like love for others, and wants nothing more than to lift them up, and cheer them on toward spiritual maturity. The mentor has the unique vision and insight for how best to connect with the broken. Once you're called into action by the Holy Spirit, take the hint. Don't be afraid to step out in faith. Once you accept your new role as a parent mentor, God will be with you every step of the way.

There may be times when the one in your spiritual care wavers or wanders off the path. But it is your duty to be patient, to be supportive while gently wooing them back, and to love them unconditionally, reminding them of their identity in Christ. Many stumble on their way to maturity, but God will be there to support you, to give you the strength to carry on, and the courage to see it through, if you're willing to stay the course.

If your spiritual son or daughter falls you must offer firm yet loving correction while always communicating your love and hope for them. Be the role model they so desperately need by showing compassion rather than harsh judgment, while demonstrating your steadfast belief that God see them as winners, victorious in every area. They just need a cheerleader to urge them on, telling them they can do it.

Remember, Paul said this:

"Follow my example, as I follow the example of Christ." (1 Cor. 11:1, NIV).

When they fall away, you must pray for them and believe that God won't give up on them, but will grab hold of their hearts and restore them, as long as they repent and seek true restoration. He will heal their wounds, turn their scars into stars and give them the second chance they so desperately need. Wrap your arms around them and show them the love of Christ; weep with them, and listen to them the way few others do.

You don't have to be a biological parent to be a spiritual mother or father. Paul had no children of his own, but he went on to become the greatest example of a father the world has ever seen. Use your past life experiences to offer love, support, and guidance to someone in need.

In the end, there is no greater investment you can make than giving yourself to raise up the fallen and restore them to God. Bandage a wound, hug a neck, and love on the broken. And you may be surprised at how much you are blessed in the process, doing something that will truly count for eternity.

Lord, help me to minister to these precious wounded warriors. Give me the love, grace, kindness, gentleness, patience, encouragement, compassion, guidance and forgiveness for these dear ones. Enable me to be that spiritual parent with a tender heart to the spiritual children that have no one to love them. Help me to correct them in Love. I refuse to give up or let them go until they're whole and healed. Each and every child of God is far too valuable to the body of Christ to condemn or throw away. Lord, you have no misfits!

Moving Beyond Your Past

"No, dear brothers and sisters, I have not achieved it, but I focus on this one thing: Forgetting the past and looking forward to what lies ahead."
(Philippians 3:13)

Dear Precious One,

For the most part we human beings tend to overestimate our failures and underestimate times of success. The truth is that every fulfilled dream occurred because of dedication, fortitude and staying the course, refusing to give up. Failure does not have to shatter your dreams.

The truth is —every last one of us has failed in some way or another. Either we caused the failure or it just overtook us through no fault of our own. The question is—what are you going to do about it? Are you going to wallow in that failure forever? I hear some saying, "Steve, what if I blew it big time and it was *all* my fault?" We all have things in our past we're ashamed of, mistakes we made along the way, disasters that could have been avoided if we'd been wiser, and more careful. But my dear sister and brother, you

113

cannot go back and change a single thing. All that wishing and hoping will change nothing. ***But*, you can change your future!** You can begin today to develop a plan for your success, to learn from your failures and grow. It's time to glean wisdom from your mistakes; you can use them to bring healing to others. Stop beating yourself up over your past! It's time to throw away the rear view mirror and reach toward your God-given destiny. To change your future, you must first change your attitude about the past.

Try these keys:

- See yourself as you are. Study both your positive and negative character traits.

- Be transparent and own your past blunders honestly, out loud to a trusted friend. Ask God to cleanse and purify your heart.

- Determine your strengths and build on them with great passion.

- Leave the past in the past. *No* more beating yourself up, because you can't change the past—only your future. Forgive yourself.

- Ask people you trust to honestly evaluate your weaknesses and strengths. Stay accountable to others.

- Create a plan that will build on your strengths and help you reach your God-given destiny.

- Shake off the dirt and begin again! Start today!

Remember; if you've never failed you probably never put yourself out there. Life always brings risks and the potential to blow it big time. Don't excuse your failures or underestimate them, but learn and glean integrity and strength from them. You may possibly make occasional blunders and disappoint others, but you should get back up and learn the lessons you need to from them, then repent with all your heart and move on.

Carrying shame the rest of your life will only rob you of your destiny. Press on in your holy calling! Keep your eye on the goal, where God is beckoning you onward—to Jesus. Take off running and do not turn back again.

It was John Maxwell who said in his book, *Failing Forward*:

"Remember that adversity creates resilience, develops maturity, builds character, pushes you to give your best performance, provides greater opportunities, prompts innovation, and reveals unexpected benefits. Sometimes a mistake can be the million-dollar idea or invention like Ivory soap or Kellogg's Corn Flakes, products which were both created by accident.

Adversity motivates. Lose your job once and bounce back by finding a new and better one. Lose that new job and start your own business. The business fails and you move to another town and find a wonderful new job in a different field. It just takes a positive, optimistic attitude to get through the bad times, because these things, too, will pass. Work hard at your action plan and think ahead.

Learn from all your experiences whether good or bad. Nothing can teach you better than a bad experience."

Child of God, take a risk and move forward with your dreams. Failure does not have to defeat your future. In fact, if you glean wisdom and new direction from your past mistakes, you can make your future a beautiful thing to behold!

Lord, I do not excuse my failures or underestimate them, but I choose to learn from them and glean integrity and strength from them. I repent for hurting your heart, but I will get back up again and learn the wisdom I need. I will not carry shame the rest of my life and allow that to rob me of my purpose and divine destiny. I choose to press on toward the mark of the high calling!

You are Coming out of that PIT!

He lifted me out of the slimy pit, out of the mud and mire; he set my feet on a rock and gave me a firm place to stand. (Psalms 40:2)

Dear Precious One,

One morning, in prayer, I saw a giant pit that had trapped many people—a pit of despair, of sin, of compromise, of failure and hopelessness. Then I saw the Great Shepherd extend His hand to pull OUT desperate souls, giving them a second chance and making all things new!

I believe that in the church there is coming a season of tremendous **restoration and preparation,** for God desires to restore all that the locust has eaten in your life! He will give you double for your trouble and turn your scars into stars reversing the curse. Let me emphasize here that this is a strategic season and we are not to squander or waste it.

The Lord says, *"This season, if you will hear My words—you will come out of that pit, so do not be content to stay there.*

Do not lose hope and accept your desperate situation, but rather speak to your pit, to your circumstances, and say, "I am coming out!" Satan has tried to manipulate and deceive, convincing many that there is no way out of the pit, and when they believe his words, they become apathetic and lose hope. But his words are lies, because you are coming up and out!

This season is a strategic one and you MUST invest and be a good steward of this time, in order to be prepared for what is coming in the near future. Do not say, "I have another year to get it together," or "I will worry about that later." Now is the time! You have a choice—will you accept your fate and remain in your pit, or will you take the hand of the Great Shepherd who desires to pull you out and once again set your feet on solid rock?

The years ahead are incredibly important, and the choice you make now will determine your course. I hear the Lord say even now: *"Will you waste another year? Will you squander it, staying in that pit of hopelessness? I am already reaching out to you, so take My hand, and let Me pull you out and give you a second chance! I am calling you! Come out and be separate! Do not dabble in the world. Do not flirt with compromise and sin, for Satan knows his time is short, and that what he does he must do quickly. Be not ignorant of his evil plans toward you, but know that I have already provided a way of escape for you."*

I hear the Great Shepherd saying, *"I am calling the prodigals home, so stop running! Can you hear Me calling your name?*

Can you sense My great love for you even now? For I have a table prepared just for you—a place already set, and I am inviting you to come and fellowship with Me again at My table. Remember when we would sit there for hours sharing our hearts with each other? I miss My time with you! I'm calling you home right now. Do not feel shame, guilt, or fear, but COME as you are and I will lovingly restore you for I am God. DO NOT WAIT ANY LONGER! I have already prepared a feast for you, as well as a new set of royal robes, and right now I give you a rod of authority. I will restore you, and you will reclaim all!"

"But while he was still a long way off, his father saw him and was filled with compassion for him; he ran to his son, threw his arms around him and kissed him." (Luke 15: 20)

Beloved, if you have a son, daughter, or loved one who is a prodigal, declare that this is your season! Don't give up! Don't accept the lies of the enemy. LOOK UP and declare that this is your year of total restoration!

In this season, I also see the Lord's hand pulling out many believers who are trapped in the pit of debt and sickness, the pit of lost opportunity, the pit of depression, delivering them from strongholds and carnal habits. This new season will also be that of *preparation* for that which is ahead, that is why this word is so vital; we MUST be prepared! We stand at a crossroads. There will be a great and terrible divide between those who are hungry for God and those who are spiritually content in their apathy.

"But while they were on their way to buy the oil, the bridegroom arrived. The virgins who were ready went in with him to the wedding banquet. And the door was shut." (Matthew 25:10)

There will be a great divide between the *"wise virgins"* of Matthew 25 and the *"foolish ones."* And while the apathetic spirit of Laodicea (see Rev. 3:14-22) will increase there will also be a *growing* remnant who will seek God's heart, and refuse to compromise or accept anything less than His fullness and the manifest presence of God.

I see desperate ones coming out of the pit of Laodicea; I see them fully abandoning themselves for the deeper things of God. And they will not be left empty-handed, but God will fill their treasures with Himself and they will feast on His presence, becoming mighty warriors equipped with everything they need for the most powerful ministry the world has ever seen! Let your kingdom come, Oh Lord!

I thank you, Lord, that this next season in my life will be one of restoration and preparation! I look up from the pit and see my Redeemer that stands with eyes full of love ready to pull me out and give me a fresh start. Let me hear you whisper my name and let me sense your loving touch. Oh, how You love us, beloved. Oh, how you love us all!

The Lord is saying, "Mighty Warrior, come out of that pit!"

Flooded with Divine Love

*"19 [That you may really come] to know
[practically, through experience for yourselves] the
love of Christ, which far surpasses mere knowledge
[without experience]; that you may be filled [through
all your being] unto all the fullness of God [may
have the richest measure of the divine Presence,
and become a body wholly filled and flooded with God
Himself]!" (Ephesians 3:19, AMP)*

Dear Precious One,

From deep inside me springs a heartfelt prayer—that
you will be filled with the amazing love of Christ—that
His love will strengthen you and help you through the
darkest nights of your battles. You are not alone, nor are
you forgotten. In fact, He holds you ever so close. This
amazing love wants to fill you with all you need, giving
you an inner strength to lead you out of the deep, dark
forest of confusion and bring you safely home. He is your
Beacon of Hope!

Jesus himself is inviting you into divine relationship, a sweeter communion where His tender affection is poured like a healing balm into all the broken places of your heart. I see Him taking the broken pieces in His hands and breathing new life into them, so you can begin again. He wants you to become deeply rooted in His love and discover the extravagant dimensions of His heart for you. Reach out and take His hand—He's waiting for you even now. As you rest there, test its length, fathom the depth, and rise to the heights of His tender affection for you, filled to overflowing!

I'm not talking about a mere intellectual grasp of His love, but rather a divine personal revelation that comes only through experience. Not just a documenting of facts or data gleaned from information, but through a personal encounter as His beauty is revealed to you, transforming you one revelation at a time, making you confident of your identity in Him, and strengthening and maturing you for the long haul.

You see, He's already with you, eager to fill you with His loving presence—a presence that has the power to set you free, to heal your wounds, and to give you a fresh start. He won't tease you with just a tiny taste, but rather a massive dose of His life and love. He's a generous Father who doesn't hold Himself back from those He loves, especially those who seek Him with their whole hearts.

Are you ready to be flooded by His presence—to have your entire being completely saturated with the fullness of God? In His fullness He'll let you touch His face, see His power, and even let you feel His tender mercies pouring over you. In that place you'll discover what it means to belong to Christ personally, and dwell in a place where His eyes actually penetrate the darkness of your heart and shatter its power over you.

> **"All glory to him who loves us and has freed us from our sins by shedding his blood for us."**
> ***(Revelation 1:5b)***

When we were still only an idea in the mind of God, the Lord had already memorized our faces and planned our redemption: **"According as he hath chosen us in him before the foundation of the world, that we should be holy and without blame before him in love."** (Ephesians 1:4) Before you ever became wounded in the battle, our *God was already planning your healing and comeback!* Did you get that?

To what extent does God adore you? He's cherished you since before time began—in fact, He is love—it's His very identity. It's in His DNA. He adored you when you turned your back on Him. He adored you in the womb. There was no beginning to His adoration for you, and it has no limits—none at all!

When will God stop loving you? He could no more stop loving you than He could stop loving His own Son, Jesus. John 13:1 says, **"The Father, having loved his own which were in the world, he loved them unto the end."**

123

There's a whole ocean of His love for you to cleanse in. A flood of divine love found in His glorious presence is headed your way. May you find divine healing and blessed hope there as you bask in His fullness, where He breathes new life into the broken pieces inside you, making you brand new!

I am not alone, nor am I forgotten. In fact, You hold me ever so close. This amazing love wants to fill me with all I need, giving me an inner strength that will plant my feet on solid ground again. Thank you, sweet Master!

A Prophetic Word

"Wait on the LORD: be of good courage, and he shall strengthen thine heart: wait, I say, on the LORD."
(Psalms 27:14)

My Tender Child,

Calamity of Heart, you cry! "All is lost and my heart is weak and broken. If you could peel the skin back to expose everything underneath, the world would plainly see the damage afflicting my soul."

Right now My word to you is alive and powerful if you will respond to it. It is sharper than the sharpest two-edged sword, cutting between soul and spirit, between joint and marrow. **This word has quickening power—you are to "Wait on Me..."**

Yes, wait on Me. Hold your wounded heart out to Me and I will strengthen you. As you hold still and allow my Spirit to calm your fears and worries I will pour over you healing oil. Be of good courage, for I am gracious, slow to anger and abounding in love. I will show myself faithful and powerful in mending your heart—only come and wait on Me to touch you. **'Be still and know that I am God!'** (Psalms 46:10)

Do not rush this process. Let rivers of living water flow over the scarred places of your heart, until I fill your heart with My tender love that heals and restores as nothing else can.

When I begin to blow My healing breath upon your heart you will feel like you are coming alive and will be tempted to run back out to the battlefield prematurely. Hold steady and refuse to budge from that secret place of waiting until I give you the signal. Then you will be a mighty warrior—ready, eager and empowered to win!

Rhema Cheswan 18, 5783

As you wait and hold still I will do a deep work in you. Like a skilled surgeon who cuts away the infected parts, I will cut away all anger, bitterness, resentment, and carnal works of the flesh. I will remove every harmful thing from within your soul while cleansing you with healing waters.

'And I will give you a new heart, and I will put a new spirit in you. I will take out your stony, stubborn heart and give you a tender, responsive heart' so you more closely reflect the heart of your Heavenly Daddy. (Ezekiel 36:26)

The healing process is critical, so let me stress again, do not rush Me. Only wait and watch your Great Physician and Healer restore you to perfect health. You will become my masterpiece! I am not through with you, so stay put, and patiently wait for My healing water to saturate and restore you. My water will purify you and set you apart for Myself, giving you a heart of flesh for a heart of stone, so you can work in unity with Me, and together we can change the world!

Dear Reader,

If your life was touched while reading *Streams in the Desert* please let us know! We would love to celebrate with you! Please visit our website, www.findrefuge.tv

Consumed by His Presence,

Steve Porter

* We invite you to read the companion book: **He Leads Me Beside Still Waters-** *50 Love Letters of Healing and Restoration from our Lord*

Deeper Life
PRESS

More books by Steve Porter

Crocodile Meat- *New and Extended Version*

Crocodile Meat- *Student Version*

Whispers from the Throne Room- *Reflections on the Manifest Presence*

Limitless

He Leads Me Beside Still Waters- *50 Love Letters of Healing and Restoration from our Lord*

Streams in the Desert- *Healing Letters for the Wounded Heart*

Invading the Darkness - *Power Evangelism Training 101*

Coming in 2016

Pearls of His Presence-*Intimate Devotions for the Spirtual Hungry*

Draw Me- *The Cry of the Bride*

More books by Deeper Life Press

Walter Beuttler- *My Spiritual Journey*

For more info see our website

www.findrefuge.tv

Contact Info
Refuge Ministries
P.O Box 381
Bloomfield, NY 14469
<u>www.findrefuge.tv</u>
Rescue. Restore. Revive